D0560961

Millard Fillmore

13th President of the United States

A conservative, careful man who strove to preserve the Union, Millard Fillmore became the 13th President of the United States after the unexpected death of Zachary Taylor. His term was marked by political turmoil, compromise, and economic expansion. (Library of Congress.)

Millard Fillmore

13th President of the United States

Kevin J. Law

GEC GARRETT EDUCATIONAL CORPORATION

Manufactured in the United States of America

Edited and produced by Synthegraphics Corporation

Library of Congress Cataloging in Publication Data

Law, Kevin.
  Millard Fillmore, 13th president of the United States / Kevin Law.
    p.   cm. — (Presidents of the United States)
  Includes bibliographical references.
  Summary: Examines the life of Millard Fillmore from birth to death, including his childhood, education, and political career.
  1. Fillmore, Millard, 1800–1874—Juvenile literature. 2. Presidents—United States—Biography—Juvenile literature. 3. United States—Politics and government—1849–1853—Juvenile literature. [1. Fillmore, Millard, 1800–1874. 2. Presidents.]   I. Title II. Series.
E427.L38   1990
973.6'4'092—dc20   64737
[B]
[92]   89-25651
                                                 CIP
                                                  AC

Contents

Chronology for Millard Fillmore

1800   Born on January 7 in Locke Township, New York

1814–
1815   Apprenticed as a wool carder and cloth dresser

1819–
1822   Studied law in Montville and Buffalo, New York

1823   Admitted to the New York bar

1826   Married Abigail Powers on February 6

1828–
1832   Served in the New York State Assembly

1832–
1834   Served one term in the U.S. House of Representatives

1836–
1842   Served in U.S. House of Representatives for three consecutive terms

1848   Served as comptroller of New York State; elected Vice-President of the United States in November

1850   Became President on July 10 following death of Zachary Taylor

1852   Lost nomination as Whig presidential candidate

1853   Wife died on March 30

1856   Presidential candidate for the Know-Nothing Party

1858   Married Caroline Carmichael MacIntosh on February 10

1874   Died on March 8 in Buffalo, New York

Chapter 1

An Ambition for Distinction

A strikingly handsome young man, nattily dressed in a stovepipe hat and carrying a pearl-handled walking stick, stepped off the stagecoach platform onto the wooden sidewalk in front of Albany's elegant Delevan House Hotel. Bracing himself against a frigid December wind, he gazed wonderingly up and down the unpaved street. Even though the street was nearly empty and no one was watching, he tried hard not to gawk, so as not to betray his awe at what he saw.

Here, in New York's second-largest city, the man felt like the country boy that he really was. The only other city he had ever seen was Buffalo, New York, a fledgling community on the banks of Lake Erie. But in contrast to Buffalo's flimsy wooden buildings and open fields, Albany's streets were lined with solid brick and stone buildings crowded together to give an impression of sturdiness and density.

THE NEW ASSEMBLYMAN

Summoning up all the confidence he could muster, the young man strode briskly into the hotel lobby. There he sought out the proprietor and, with a suavity befitting his appearance,

1

announced himself as Millard Fillmore, recently elected New York state assemblyman from Erie County.

Bystanders in the hotel lobby could hardly have guessed that this polished young gentleman, then 29 years old, had not been born to wealth and gracious living. He looked so poised and comfortable in his fine clothes, and handled his cane with such grace, that only the most careful observer could have seen any sign of his humble background.

In reality, however, young Millard's transformation from farmer's son to state legislator had been gradual and difficult, accomplished with almost no formal training or education. As a boy he had dreamed of fame and decided early that farm labor was not for him. It wasn't the hard work but, rather, the degrading nature of manual labor that he disliked. He also hated his father's poverty and promised himself that he would do everything he could to improve his position in life.

Millard was now on his way. But little in his background justified the air of quiet confidence that surrounded him. It was more stage presence than natural composure, fired by an intense ambition to succeed.

HUMBLE BEGINNINGS

Ambition was a quality deeply ingrained in young Millard. In 1799, one year before his birth, his parents, Nathaniel and Phoebe Fillmore, had joined a great westward migration in search of opportunity and a better life. The Fillmores were just two of the many thousands of brave, hopeful Americans who settled in central and western New York—just recently the site of bloody Indian wars.

During the Revolutionary War, New York had set aside almost 1½ million acres of land in the central part of the state.

The plan was to present parcels to qualified veterans as war bonuses. But few war veterans ever settled in the area, known as the Military Tract. Instead, real estate speculators gained title to much of the land—mostly through the favors of corrupt government officials. Sales agents for these speculators traveled far and wide, looking for customers.

In Bennington, Vermont, one unscrupulous sales agent found Nathaniel Fillmore working a rocky plot of farmland that yielded little and promised little for a lifetime of back-breaking toil. Lured by the agent's reports of a fertile paradise in the Military Tract, Nathaniel and his brother Calvin purchased—sight unseen—a piece of land in Locke Township, Cayuga County, New York.

As farmers, Nathaniel and Calvin expected to have to work hard to turn their new plot into a prosperous farm. As soon as they arrived, they set to work clearing fields, planting seeds, and building a cabin for their families. But their high expectations proved ill-founded. Instead of fertile loam, the Fillmore brothers found hard, infertile clay. And instead of prosperity, they found more poverty.

The Birth of a President

On the morning of January 7, 1800, in a small log cabin separated from its nearest neighbor by four miles of snow-covered forest, a son was born to Nathaniel and Phoebe Fillmore. (They already had one daughter, Olive Armstrong Fillmore, born in 1797.) In their joy, the new parents momentarily forgot their desperate condition and turned their attention to selecting a name for the boy. After much discussion, they finally chose a name that expressed their devotion to each other. They named their son Millard, Phoebe's maiden name.

Unfortunately, Millard's birth was only a brief distraction from the Fillmore's mounting troubles. To the problems of poor soil, poor crops, and a crowded cabin was added a faulty land title—a common problem in those days in the Military Tract and throughout the American frontier. Inaccurate land surveys, claim-jumping, ignorance, and plain dishonesty had made such a mess of the Tract's land titles that the state of New York had to send a team of commissioners to review all the land titles in the region.

Because the Fillmore brothers were unable to defend their ownership against the commissioners' findings, they lost their property. Disheartened, they packed their families and their few belongings on a farm wagon and moved a few miles south to Sempronius (now called Niles), about one mile west of Lake Skaneateles in what is now known as New York's Finger Lakes region. Here, instead of settling on their own land, the Fillmores took a perpetual lease on a 130-acre farm and became tenant farmers.

Boyhood Days

Millard spent his childhood on this farm, on the edge of civilization in the woodlands of New York. As a farmer, his father worked hard, and even as a young child Millard was expected to do his share of the chores. Early on, he learned how to hoe corn, mow hay, and reap wheat. As he grew older and stronger, he spent many days guiding a wooden plow behind a pulling mule. During the long cold winters, he cut and hauled the logs for the farmhouse fireplace. In the warmer months, he cleared new cropland, cutting trees, burning brush, and pulling stumps.

By the time Millard reached the age of 15, he was a strong, husky young man who had mastered nearly every aspect of frontier farming. Only occasionally was he able to steal away to the woods for some hunting or to the shores of Lake Skaneateles for some fishing. But every time he did, his father would lecture him on the evils of such idleness. "No man," he would intone, "ever prospered from wasting his time in sporting."

In Nathaniel Fillmore's eyes, hunting and fishing were suitable pastimes only for Indians and white good-for-nothings; civilization was a serious matter that demanded hard work and ambition. He was determined that if he could not succeed, then he would do everything in his power to see that his oldest son succeeded.

A Young Apprentice

But in truth, Millard's rise from his humble beginnings owed as much to his father's failures as to his own ambition. Plagued again by poor soil, Nathaniel continued to struggle as a tenant farmer, although his family continued to grow (to nine children in all, five boys and four girls). He vowed that none of his five sons would have to struggle at so unrewarding an occupation as farming.

Because Nathaniel lacked the money to send his sons to school to train for professional careers, he apprenticed them to tradesmen, at no cost, to learn trades. When Millard was 14, he was apprenticed to a clothmaker, Benjamin Hungerford, of Sparta, New York. One of his duties was wool-carding, a task he especially hated. After only four months of working for the ill-tempered Mr. Hungerford, young Millard quit and returned home. Nathaniel soon found Millard another apprenticeship, this time with clothmakers Zaccheus Chaney and Alvan Kellogg in New Hope, New York. Here, Millard spent several years, and grew from boy to man.

A HUNGER FOR KNOWLEDGE

As Millard tended the mill machines, he became painfully aware of his ignorance. Although he had taken all the schooling Cayuga County could offer, he still had only basic knowledge of reading, writing, and mathematics. He loved to read, but few books were available besides the Bible and a few spelling and reading primers. Years later, looking back, Fillmore described his family library as "a Bible, a hymn book, and an almanac."

But Millard had a hunger for knowledge and, at age 17, when a library was started in the community, he joined. He attacked the books voraciously and discovered a whole world of ideas that he had never been exposed to. But he soon became frustrated by his small vocabulary, which limited his understanding of the books he read. Showing his determination to learn, he bought a dictionary and began to learn the meaning of every new word. He set up a desk in the cloth mill and, in spare moments, looked up a new word and fixed the meaning in his memory.

Schooling and Love

Soon came the chance for an education that Millard had dreamed of. An enterprising teacher opened an "academy" in New Hope, near the mill. Although it was only a pale replica of the old eastern academies, such as Groton, Exeter, and Deerfield, the new school far surpassed anything young Fillmore had known. Taking advantage of a slack season at the mill, he enrolled in the school.

Millard gloried in the new school experience. For the first time, he saw a map, learned formal grammar—and began to experience the pleasures of female company. Abigail

Powers was 21; he was 19. She was his teacher; he was her willing pupil. But more than just age and education separated them. She was the daughter of a prominent local preacher and the sister of a judge; he was the son of a poor tenant farmer.

But the social gap that separated Millard and Abigail was too small to discourage them from first becoming friends and then falling in love. They spent much time together in the winter of 1819, but in the spring the progress of their love was interrupted by a new opportunity for Millard.

A SURPRISE

Once again Nathaniel Fillmore intervened in his son's life — this time, however, with more beneficial results. While Millard was courting Abigail in New Hope, Nathaniel was plotting a new career for him. After 17 years of fruitless struggle with clayey soil, Nathaniel sold his tenancy in Sempronius and moved the family about a dozen miles southwest to Montville, New York, where he became a tenant of Judge Walter Wood.

Then in his 70s, old Judge Wood was one of the region's wealthiest men. His law practice prospered on the land title litigation that flooded the Military Tract, and he ran his business with a cold, shrewd eye on the bottom line. Seeing an opportunity, Nathaniel persuaded the judge to try out Millard for two months as a clerk in his law office.

Millard knew nothing about the arrangements until he returned home from New Hope. The first evening at the dinner table, his proud mother suddenly and unexpectedly announced the news. Overcome with emotion, Millard burst into tears of joy. Then, embarrassed by his unmanly display, he bolted from the table.

Early the next morning Millard reported to Judge Wood's office, eager to begin. The wrinkled old man greeted him perfunctorily, shoved the first volume of Blackstone's *Commentaries* (a famous English law text) into his hands, and directed, "Thee will please turn thy attention to this."

OPPORTUNITY KNOCKS

In June, after the two-month trial with Judge Wood had passed, Millard sadly packed his few belongings and prepared to make the journey back to New Hope to resume his apprenticeship in the cloth mill. Although he had spent only two months as a student clerk and found the study of English law difficult, he had grown to like the position. More important, he had come to appreciate what a law career could offer him: money, prestige, and security. In contrast, the cloth mill seemed to promise nothing but struggle and despair.

But Millard had no reason to believe that Judge Wood would encourage him to continue. After all, the sour-faced old judge had seldom commented on his work. As Millard prepared to say good-bye, however, the judge startled him by announcing, "If thee has an ambition for distinction, and can sacrifice everything else to success, the law is the road that leads to honors; and if thee can get rid of thy engagement to serve as an apprentice, I would advise thee to come back again and study law."

Instead of joy, despair showed on Millard's face. Knowing that he faced seven years as a law clerk before he could be admitted to the bar and begin practice, he sadly informed the judge, "I have no means of paying my way." With uncharacteristic generosity, the judge came to Millard's aid. "I can give thee some employment in attending to my business in the country," he offered, "and if necessary I will advance thee some money and thee can repay it when thee gets into practice."

Arranging a Buy-Out

Seeing the chance to begin fulfilling his ambitions, Millard accepted Judge Wood's offer and arranged to buy his way out of his apprenticeship. Since he still had two years of the apprenticeship to serve, he struck a bargain with the mill owners, Chaney and Kellogg, in which he agreed to give up any salary due him and pay an additional $30 to gain his release. He then returned to Sempronius and took a job teaching in the town's new elementary school. After three months he had earned the $30 he needed to pay off the mill owners.

Free at last to pursue his chosen career, Millard hurried back to Judge Wood's office in Montville and began studying law in earnest. He also worked on changing his image. Soon he had discarded his rough cowhide boots for fine leather shoes and was wearing suits and high white collars. He even started to carry a cane — in his mind, the mark of a true gentleman. Suddenly, he was no longer Millard, the lowly clothmaker's apprentice — he was now Mr. Fillmore, promising and stylish young law clerk.

For more than two years, young Millard Fillmore worked for and studied law with Judge Walter Wood in Montville, New York. One of his duties was helping the judge oversee his many tenant farms. (Library of Congress.)

Chapter 2

Entry into Politics

The course to Millard's law career did not run very smoothly. One of his tasks was to help Judge Wood oversee his many tenant farms scattered over several counties in the Military Tract. In this position, working closely with the judge, Millard observed the judge's business methods—and did not like what he saw. He found the judge too cold and calculating, with little compassion for his tenant's problems and suffering. Many times Millard had to perform the unpleasant task of evicting a poor tenant family from one of Judge Wood's farms. Soon Millard himself was to fall victim to the harsh, demanding judge.

FIRST LAWSUIT

One day in the autumn of 1821, a local farmer involved in a minor lawsuit offered Millard three dollars to represent him before a justice of the peace. Millard eagerly accepted, anxious to have a little money for himself that he did not have to borrow from Judge Wood. So eager was Millard to do something on his own that he did not seem to be concerned about his inexperience and ignorance of many aspects of the law. Fortunately, he was able to conceal this ignorance by settling the lawsuit out of court.

An Angry Judge

But when Judge Wood heard of the matter, he angrily reprimanded Millard. He forbade Millard to ever practice before a justice of the peace again, stating that such practice could ruin Millard's career as a lawyer by corrupting him with the slang and slipshod procedures of common justice-of-the-peace cases. Although Millard pleaded that he needed the money and the experience that such cases provided, the judge was adamant. He demanded Millard's promise not to do it again.

As Millard stood before the irate judge, his mind filled with an image of the judge's greedy, grasping hand reaching out to capture him and take control of his life. To Millard, the judge was "more anxious to keep me in a state of dependence and use me as a drudge in his business than to make a lawyer of me."

Filled with more than a little righteous rage, Millard felt that his rights were being violated. He found Judge Wood's greed and coldness suddenly too repulsive to tolerate. Despite the great harm that such a move undoubtedly would cause his law career, he felt that he had no choice but to leave the judge. So he quit and, leaving a note indicating that he owed the judge $65, prepared to rejoin his father on the farm.

A PERIOD OF DESPAIR

Millard returned to his family in a state of deep despair at what he thought was the end of his law career. Nathaniel Fillmore, meanwhile, had given up trying to make a go of farming in central New York. Once again he uprooted the family, this time moving westward to Aurora Township, some 18 miles east of Buffalo, New York, in Erie County.

As he settled in his parents' farmhouse, Millard, now 21, saw his future stretching emptily before him. Although during that winter he handled a few justice-of-the-peace cases for relatives and neighbors and taught school in East Aurora, he was "very much discouraged." All he could do was "hope, like Micawber [a character in Charles Dickens' *David Copperfield,* known for his unflagging optimism in the face of disaster] that something would turn up."

A Chance for Success

Once again, however, Nathaniel Fillmore had, through his restlessness, unwittingly aided Millard. His move to Aurora Township, with its proximity to the emerging city of Buffalo, greatly enhanced his son's chance for success. But at first, Millard could not see the advantage of living near Buffalo. His memories of the city were less than fond. In May 1818, when he was 17 years old, Millard had taken advantage of a slow period at the cloth mill to "see the country." He shouldered a knapsack and hiked the 140 miles from Sempronius to Buffalo, where he visited some relatives in the nearby village of Wales.

He made this journey just 4½ years after the British had burned Buffalo during the War of 1812. At that time, he reported later, the community:

> . . . presented a straggling appearance. It was just rising from the ashes and there were many cellars and chimneys without houses, showing that its destruction by the British had been complete. My feet had become blistered, and I was very sore in every joint and muscle; and I suffered intensely. I crossed the . . . Indian reservation to Aurora, and recollect a long

rotten causeway of logs extending across the low ground from
Seneca Street nearly to the creek, over which I paddled myself in a canoe. I [stayed] all night at a kind of Indian tavern
about six miles from Buffalo. . . . A number of drunken Indians and white men kept up a row during most of the night.
Next day I went through the woods alone to Wales.

Boomtown

By 1822, however, Buffalo had changed dramatically. Its inhabitants had repaired the damage done by the British and
the city was now in the middle of a building boom that would
extend far into the future. Already it had more than 300 buildings and 4,000 people.

In addition, work on the western end of the Erie Canal,
New York's great inland canal system, was set to begin near
Buffalo the following year. In anticipation of this important
transportation link, harbor and shipyard construction began
along Lake Erie. All this growth seemed to guarantee Buffalo's prosperity, and speculators scrambled for land and construction contracts, creating an atmosphere of activity and
excitement.

Swept up in this atmosphere on a visit in the spring of
1822, Millard instantly changed his attitude toward Buffalo.
Suddenly, his life seemed to have exciting new possibilities.
Never before had he seen so many people living together—
so many different kinds of people! Up to now he had known
mainly farmers. Rubbing shoulders with merchants, hotel
keepers, lake captains, canal workers, and others of varied
and colorful backgrounds and experience gave Millard a new
outlook on life. Many travelers from abroad who visited Buffalo and other emerging areas of the American frontier complained about—as one Englishman put it—its "crude,

undisciplined inhabitants" who seemed "caught up in a mad scramble for wealth." But to Millard, Buffalo was an exotic, sophisticated land of possibility. He took a teaching position, then set out to absorb Buffalo's atmosphere and become a part of it.

ON TRACK AGAIN

Millard's move to Buffalo rekindled his ambition—and hopes—for a law career. For Buffalo's growth had brought more than a dozen law firms to the city and surrounding Erie County, and law clerks were in high demand. In the summer of 1822, Millard entered the law firm of Asa Rice and Joseph Clary as a clerk.

By agreement with his new employers, Millard kept his teaching position and devoted almost all his spare time and summer months working as a clerk and studying law. This arrangement was ideal. Teaching paid for Millard's living expenses, and the law work allowed him to meet Buffalo's business and political leaders.

Gradually, Millard impressed himself on these leaders. He cultivated the qualities that he admired in others—serious attitude, decorous (correct) bearing, temperate (sober) habits, orthodox (established) opinions—and gained their notice and approval. He worked hard in the law office and the classroom, devoting himself to the law even more fervently than to mastering the social graces. Early on, his solid and steady character were apparent to all those who came in contact with him, and his circle of important associates grew rapidly. He became so well known for sound judgment that the phrase "If Millard Fillmore goes for it, so do I" soon was in wide use throughout Buffalo.

A Lawyer at Last

Millard's influential new circle of friends included several older lawyers who recognized the young clerk's potential. These lawyers persuaded the new Erie County Court of Common Pleas to approve Millard's entry to law practice. In 1823, within just a year of joining the firm of Rice and Clary, Millard was admitted to the New York bar—a lawyer at last!

But although overjoyed at reaching his goal, Millard was also troubled by a nagging anxiety. For beneath his new-found sophistication and suavity lay a deep modesty and a bit of insecurity. Even though he was now a lawyer, he still had many gaps in his knowledge of law and little experience in practice. His training encompassed only about 27 months instead of the usual seven years. Feeling unsure of his legal skills, he turned down an offer of a partnership with one of his former employers, Joseph Clary. Instead, he returned to East Aurora and opened the village's first law office.

A Time for Growth and Learning

To Millard's family and friends, his return to East Aurora hardly seemed like a wise move. How, they wondered, could he leave his promising future in one of New York's most bustling cities for an uncertain practice in quiet, lazy East Aurora? Years later, in his memoirs, Millard explained, "Not having sufficient confidence in myself to enter into competition with the older members of the Bar . . . I opened an office in East Aurora."

Millard's practice consisted mainly of simple cases involving matters such as land titles, mortgages, and debt collections. He charged reasonable fees, and his income was small but adequate. Quickly, the same dedication and personal qualities that drew attention and admiration in Buffalo began to serve him well in East Aurora and the surrounding area. He gained increasing confidence in his professional and social abilities. At only 23, he became the village's leading citizen and helped set its social and political tone.

The young lawyer's growing reputation for hard work and integrity helped him gain his first governmental appointment, as the region's commissioner of deeds. The brisk pace at which speculators bought and sold real estate holdings created the need for many new deeds and deed changes. The fees Millard received for recording these deeds increased his income substantially. But this first public office, although certainly enhancing Millard's income and local influence, foretold little of the distinguished political career to come.

Romance and Marriage

After two years of practice in East Aurora, Millard finally felt confident in his ability to earn a comfortable living and support a family. He decided to fulfill the promise he had made six years earlier to Abigail Powers. They had not seen each other since Millard's admission to the bar, but their affection had survived the long separation.

As befitted a successful man, Millard traveled by stagecoach to Moravia, New York, for his reunion with Abigail. Their meeting was as joyous as they both had anticipated, and, on February 6, 1826, Reverend Orsanius H. Smith joined Abigail Powers and Millard Fillmore in marriage. The newlyweds immediately returned to East Aurora.

As it had in 1819, Abigail's love now spurred Millard to greater ambitions. The feelings of inadequacy that trou-

On February 6, 1826, in Moravia, New York, Millard Fillmore married Abigail Powers, who had been his teacher back in 1819. (Library of Congress.)

bled him in Buffalo, although still present, were greatly diminished. He strove even harder to overcome them by resolving to learn as much as possible about the legal profession. Purchasing and studying volume after volume of law texts, he applied himself religiously to mastering the intricacies of the law.

The Young Lawyer

Once again, Millard's hard work and dedication paid quick dividends. Within a year after his marriage, he had progressed enough to be admitted as an attorney, then a counselor, to the New York State Supreme Court. This appointment brought more complex legal cases and more wealthy and influential clients to his office in East Aurora. As his reputation spread, he began to attract clients from outside Erie County, from as far away as Cattaraugus and Genesee counties.

Millard soon realized that he needed help to manage his rapidly expanding practice. The overworked lawyer hired young, gangly Nathan K. Hall, a family friend from Wales, as a student clerk. To Millard, this event more than any other made him feel as if he had finally "arrived" as a lawyer. He was a teacher again, but this time in his chosen profession.

Declining a Partnership

During the years that Millard spent in East Aurora, his Buffalo friends and associates had not forgotten him. Prominent lawyers closely followed his career, which by now had brought him to argue cases before the State Supreme Court and Court of Appeals. One of these lawyers, Philander Bennett, was so impressed with Millard's ability that he offered Millard a partnership.

Although Millard considered Bennett's offer, he decided to decline it. His practice in East Aurora was too comfortable for the moment. His East Auroran neighbors liked to gather in his office—a remodeled outbuilding a few yards from his home—to pass the time of day and discuss politics and other matters. Business was good, and his status in the community climbed.

His happiness increased when, on April 28, 1828, Abigail gave birth to their first child. They named the boy Millard Powers Fillmore — not Millard, Jr., because the baby had a middle name, whereas Millard himself did not.

Up to now, Fillmore had displayed no keen interest in politics and had associated only casually with the National Republican Party. But for a young lawyer, politics held the promise of great opportunity. He would not be able to resist the lure of his ambitions for long. Gradually and steadily, they drew him toward his future.

ANTIMASON AND ASSEMBLYMAN

On the night of December 31, 1828, while most of the residents of Albany, New York, were celebrating the New Year, Millard Fillmore and 20 other sober-faced men were groping their way through the dark corridors of New York's state capitol. Flickering oil lamps lit their path as their voices echoed off the cold granite walls. This small band represented the state's emerging new political party — the Antimasons — and was gathering to plan for the upcoming session of the state legislature.

Only three years before, not one of the men could have dreamed of such a party. Most of them, like Fillmore, were newcomers to politics. Now their party controlled one-eighth of the seats in the New York state legislature, and their movement was spreading to neighboring states.

In the early 19th century, national politics were far different than they are today. Unlike now, a political party was not a powerful entity that exerted its influence through a tightly organized hierarchy extending from the national to the local level. Rather, a party was made up of many small factions, some consisting of one man's followers and few exerting influence over even an entire state. Alliances were constantly shifting, and parties could change dramatically from year to year. In this atmosphere, people did not look to a political party to stand for anything other than advancing its supporters' own interests. Moreover, restrictions on who could vote and how elections were held limited public participation in the democratic process.

The Antimason Party's Beginnings

Into this atmosphere the Antimasons burst like a fresh wind, capturing the public's imagination. The party's beginnings stemmed from a bizarre incident shrouded in mystery. In September 1826, residents of Batavia, New York, realized that they had not seen the town stonemason, William Morgan, for several days. Suspecting foul play, Morgan's wife and several other concerned citizens called for an investigation. Morgan was never found, and his fate remains unknown— although murder was suspected, and members of the Free Masons (a secret society) were implicated.

Deep in debt, Morgan had prepared a book revealing the secrets of the Ancient Order of Free Masons, of which he was a member, and was preparing to offer it for sale. He was murdered, so the theory went, to prevent him from releasing the book and revealing the Order's secrets.

As news of the incident spread, and as the contents of Morgan's book became public, a wave of anti-Masonic feelings swept through western New York and then into Pennsylvania, Vermont, and other states. In the public mind, the Ancient Order of Free Masons was an invisible empire whose

*Thurlow Weed, an influential newspaper editor first in Roches-
ter then in Albany, New York, played an important role in
Fillmore's political career—starting as a trusted ally and later
becoming a bitter enemy.* (Library of Congress.)

members had infiltrated into the highest levels of government and used their power to promote the goals of the Order – including obstructing the investigation into Morgan's disappearance. As Morgan's book revealed, the Order's secret oaths, if followed literally, indicated a total disrespect for established law and authority. Soon, a call arose from a new group, who took the name Antimasons, to purge all Masons from public office in order to restore good and just government.

Thurlow Weed

In his newspaper office in Rochester, New York, Thurlow Weed surveyed the growing political unrest with interest. As editor of the *Rochester Anti-Masonic Enquirer*, Weed had embraced the new movement heartily. But although he promoted antimasonry in his newspaper and in his political dealings, Weed really had only one goal in mind: to promote himself into a position of political power first in New York State, then in the nation at large. By age 30, he already was becoming a powerful political "boss." Over the next several decades, he was to have a profound effect on the life and career of Millard Fillmore – first as a trusted ally, later as a bitter enemy.

A Rising Politician

By the spring of 1828, Millard was in the thick of politics. In return for his support, Antimasonic leaders in Erie County made him a candidate for state assemblyman. Somewhat surprisingly, he won, drawing more votes in the county than any other candidate.

In his first year as an assemblyman, Fillmore spoke little, instead spending his time learning the intricacies of parliamentary procedure and the ways of "back-room" politics. When he returned to Albany the next year after a triumphant re-election (assemblymen served one-year terms), he was ready to take an active role in his party's future.

By 1830, Fillmore was emerging as the party leader in western New York. As he began to appear more frequently before the public, he developed a speaking style that he would use for the rest of his life. He spoke slowly and deliberately, using common words arranged in short, direct sentences. Lacking the eloquence and drama of the more accomplished public speakers of the day, Fillmore was never thought of as a great orator. Rather, he was at his best in private conversations and small groups, where his direct, clear approach was most effective.

Family Life

As Fillmore rose in political ranks, he also rose in social ranks. In the spring of 1830, he eagerly accepted an offer from Joseph Clary to join him in a law partnership and moved his family to Buffalo. The Fillmores were quickly accepted into Buffalo society. Formal dinners, chamber music recitals, dances, and the theater all crowded into their lives. They joined the Unitarian Church as charter members.

On March 27, 1832, a daughter was born to Millard and Abigail Fillmore. The proud couple named the baby Mary Abigail and called her Abby. Now their family was complete.

Chapter 3

Congressman Fillmore

As Millard Fillmore approached the outskirts of Washington, D.C., in late November 1833, he could not help but show the excitement he was feeling. Leaning forward in his carriage seat, he gazed curiously at the nation's capital. It looked not much different from the open country that he had just passed through on his journey from Baltimore, Maryland.

Along the roadside and occasionally in the road, cows paused to watch the carriage pass. Here and there, solitary farms and clumps of smaller houses broke the monotony of the landscape. Only as the carriage drew close to the center of Washington did Millard realize that there was more to the city than scattered shacks.

THE NATION'S CAPITAL

When the carriage clattered onto Pennsylvania Avenue, Fillmore caught his first full view of the national capital. The President's mansion, surrounded by the plain and imposing red brick buildings of the State, Treasury, War, and Navy departments, towered majestically over the low wooden hotels and boarding houses that lay at its feet.

This 1832 lithograph of Washington, D.C., shows the Capitol building as newly elected Congressman Fillmore might have seen it for the first time. (Library of Congress.)

As the carriage rattled down the avenue, Fillmore directed the coachman to drop him at Gadsby's, Washington's most popular and comfortable hotel. There, previous visitors had assured him, he could find a clean bed, excellent service, and a hospitable hotel-keeper. Congress was scheduled to meet in a few days, on December 2, and Millard had many things to do before he began taking up his new responsibilities.

No longer was Fillmore the timid first-term New York assemblyman who spent days gawking at Albany's streets and buildings, with no firm plan for the course of his fledgling political career. He now had no doubts about his course. He was working, with a clear vision, towards creating a new political party.

BUILDING A PARTY

Personal political ambition had little to do with Millard's new goal. Although he certainly was interested in seeking and winning election to public office, he did not need a new political organization to help him achieve this ambition. His existing political alliances had provided him with all the personal satisfaction that he sought from politics—a place in the local limelight. With their help, he had won nearly 70 percent of the vote in three successive elections for state assemblyman, and likely could be elected to virtually any office he would want to seek in western New York.

But something beyond personal ambition had taken hold of Millard Fillmore. Whatever it was—perhaps a new understanding and appreciation of the role of statesman and coalition-builder—it guided him in his work to create a new political party.

First Days in Washington

Like most new congressmen, Fillmore spent his first few days in Washington becoming acquainted with his new surroundings. He met many of his new colleagues and even some important national political figures. One night, he had the good fortune to dine in the company of the famous Senator Daniel Webster of Massachusetts. Although his political beliefs ran somewhat contrary to Webster's, Millard was impressed with the senator's warmhearted nature. Webster took an interest in Fillmore's law career, and within the month arranged for him to practice before the Supreme Court. Fillmore never forgot Webster's kindness, and in later years he also used his influence to boost many a promising young lawyer's career whenever he had the chance.

But Millard did not spend all of his time sight-seeing

and meeting luminaries such as Senator Webster. Unlike most freshman congressmen who tend to spend their first session somewhat in the background listening to the elder statesmen and taking only tentative steps toward building political alliances, Fillmore threw himself into activity. His old timidity and uncertainty were gone. Hardly had he arrived in Washington than he was sloshing through its muddy streets, enthusiastically talking to every congressman who would listen about his new party and its grand cause.

The "Panic Session"

But much other work also demanded Fillmore's attention. Washington was abuzz with news of political maneuvers. The first session of the twenty-third Congress, which convened on December 2, 1833, would go down in history as the "Panic Session." The name fit. The nation was experiencing a financial panic related to the near-collapse of the nation's largest and most powerful bank, the Bank of the United States.

Congress was split into two camps. One side, which controlled the House of Representatives, favored President Andrew Jackson, who had brought on the Bank's crisis by ordering the withdrawal of more than $12 million in government deposits from the Bank in the summer and fall of 1832. His supporters believed that Jackson had acted wisely in taking steps to limit the Bank's dominance over the nation's economy.

But the President's detractors, known to some as the Anti-Jacksons, believed that he had acted improperly and unwisely. The head of the Bank of the United States, Nicholas Biddle, became Jackson's biggest political enemy. Angered at his bank's loss of millions of dollars in government deposits and determined to thwart any further damage, Biddle set out to create a national financial panic. He used the Bank's still-vast resources to rig the nation's credit structure, and the business sector began to suffer.

By December 1833, a financial panic had begun, and for the next seven months, a hot debate swirled around Washington. The Senate, dominated by the Anti-Jacksons, was especially irate. It even censured the President for "assuming authority and power not conferred by the Constitution and laws but in derogation to them both."

Observing at some distance as the debate raged, young Congressman Fillmore regarded both sides with some disdain and misgivings. Years of experience with New York's state banking system, controlled by Martin Van Buren's powerful Democratic organization, had made him wary of large banks and their potential for gaining a financial monopoly. In fact, "down with monopoly" had been a rallying cry for the Antimasons in every election since 1829.

From Antimason to Whig

But if Fillmore could not accept the Bank of the United States, he agreed with the major purpose behind the debate about it: the creation of a national political party to strengthen the inadequate alliance of the Antimasons and the National Republicans. To build such a party required much political skill and savvy, qualities that the young congressman had in abundance.

During his first year in Congress, Fillmore threw himself into his task with great zeal. He attacked President Jackson's financial policies and made alliances with many important Antimasons and National Republicans, and even with some disgruntled Democrats. In the spring of 1834, the fledgling party entered its first election—for New York City mayor and city council seats. They also took a name—the Whigs. The newly formed Whig Party won control of the city council and lost the mayoral race by only 213 votes. The Whigs were jubilant at these results, which seemed to promise much future success.

Indeed, during the summer of 1834, the Whig movement swept westward across the country into the Ohio Valley and as far south as Louisiana. Despite resistance from some pockets of Antimasons—particularly in Pennsylvania, Vermont, Massachusetts, and, ironically, Fillmore's home territory of Erie County, New York—the new party quickly grew in size and national influence.

To Fillmore, almost everything was going according to plan. But the Erie County Antimasons, the state's stronghold of antimasonry, stubbornly resisted the entreaties to ally with the Whig Party. By midsummer 1834, Fillmore realized that his efforts to unite his supporters were futile. He also saw that without the Antimasons, the Erie County Whigs were not strong enough to elect him to another term in Congress. So he declined a Whig nomination to run for Congress and resolved to work even harder to bridge the gap between the two groups and forge a strong, lasting, politically powerful alliance.

RISE OF THE WHIGS

In early December 1834, Congressman Fillmore returned to Washington to finish his term of office. Despite his disappointment at not running for re-election, he had no intention of giving up on national politics. Instead, he threw himself even more deeply into building the Whig Party.

The Whigs were planning on entering the presidential election in 1836 and needed to field a strong candidate. Possibilities included Daniel Webster, Senator Henry Clay of Kentucky, and General William Henry Harrison of Ohio. More by default than out of admiration, Fillmore leaned toward Harrison.

Meanwhile, the political divisions in western New York still rankled Millard. After Congress adjourned, he returned home to Buffalo, determined to complete the transition of the Erie County Antimasons into the Whig Party.

The *Commercial Advertiser*

As a shrewd politician, Fillmore realized the importance of a strong newspaper to support and promote his cause. He convinced the owner of Buffalo's *Commercial Advertiser*, a daily paper that had backed the Whigs (though with not much enthusiasm), to hire a new editor — and he had just the man for the job.

Dr. Thomas A. Foote, a 24-year-old physician with a devotion to the Whigs and a talent for journalism, was a native of East Aurora, where Fillmore's parents still lived and Fillmore often visited. Fillmore had known Foote since the latter was a boy, and the two men had much respect for each others' political views and talents. For the next 20 years, Foote would remain at his editorial post as a staunch and eloquent supporter of the Whig Party and of his close friend, Millard Fillmore.

To the Rescue

With a powerful newspaper now behind him, Fillmore turned his attention to other ways of promoting the Whig Party. He soon seized upon a cause that had western New York in a turmoil. Earlier in the decade, two out-of-state land speculators, Jacob LeRoy and Heman J. Redfield, had bought large tracts of land in western New York. They instituted a harsh landlord system for their tenant farmers and extracted outrageous mortgage fees from persons who had bought land from them. Usually the victims had only the choice of paying or being evicted. Gradually, the farmers' resentment grew into hatred of LeRoy and Redfield.

The speculators, meanwhile, were having their own troubles. A state law, passed in 1832, put a tax on debt payments made to out-of-state creditors. LeRoy and Redfield exerted their considerable influence to try and have the act repealed. When they failed, they attempted to pass the expense of the tax on to their tenants and mortgagees. In the spring of 1836, the victims rebelled.

Realizing the political gains he could make from such an action, Fillmore quickly joined in the dispute on the side of the settlers. After all, he felt somewhat responsible for the affair. In his last session as a state assemblyman, he had introduced a tax bill similar to the one that was irritating the speculators.

Fillmore's bill was introduced too late for action in that session of the state assembly, but in the next session of the following year, the current bill became law. With a group of public-spirited men, Fillmore called for a meeting of the settlers to "resist the unjust oppression of the late purchasers of the Holland Purchase. . . ."

Representatives of the settlers came to Buffalo from 25 towns in Erie, Chatauqua, Genesee, and Niagara counties. Fillmore himself attended the meeting as one of Buffalo's delegates. The group adopted a long list of resolutions to present to the New York legislature, one demanding that the tax never be repealed.

Faced with mounting opposition, LeRoy and Redfield succumbed to the settlers' demands for fairer treatment. The tax remained in place. For his part in the affair, Fillmore earned the enduring gratitude of many settlers in western New York.

Fresh from this triumph, Fillmore moved to further solidify the Whig Party in the region. By the fall of 1835, he had persuaded the Antimasonic Party leaders to dissolve their Erie County organization. Their supporters had almost no choice but to join the Whigs.

BACK TO CONGRESS

Finally, the goal toward which Fillmore had been working for almost four years seemed in sight. The Whig Party had grown strong enough, in his view, to enter a candidate for the presidential election in 1836. Millard was so well satisfied with his work that in the fall of 1836 he accepted the Whig nomination for the U.S. House of Representatives, with complete confidence of victory.

Meanwhile, the Whig presidential candidate in the 1836 election had finally been chosen. William Henry Harrison was the man selected to lead the Whigs to national prominence. But the election was a disaster. Instead of unifying solidly behind Harrison, Whigs around the country split their support among four candidates — Harrison, Daniel Webster, Hugh Lawson White (a former Jacksonian from Tennessee), and Willie P. Magnum (a last-minute candidate from South Carolina). Splintered as they were, the Whigs suffered inevitable defeat, and Martin Van Buren was elected 8th President of the United States.

Fortunately for Fillmore, he experienced no problem in winning his election to a second term in Congress. But even while celebrating his victory, he was troubled by a deepening financial crisis that was affecting both Buffalo and the nation at large.

From Boom to Bust

The year 1836 saw the country in the midst of an economic boom. But it was a boom based on shaky foundation of wild speculation rather than on a solid base of economic growth. Banks all over the country issued their own currency to fuel the speculative spree. Instead of being backed by gold and silver, most of this currency was backed by nothing more than the banks' assurance of its worth. The U.S. Treasury, alarmed

This editorial cartoon, entitled "The Times," depicts the depression of 1837, showing women and children begging and living in the streets, jobless men without shoes, and a crowd around a closed bank. (Library of Congress.)

at the variety of currency it was receiving, pressured then-President Andrew Jackson to sign a bill requiring all monies paid to the federal government to be in gold or silver coin. This act made the worthlessness of most other currency apparent, and economic panic quickly swept the nation. Hundreds of banks refused to honor their own currency, and hundreds more closed their doors.

Disorder and uncertainty ruled the financial world. From one day to the next, no one was sure which bank would close or which currency would become valueless. In the midst of this chaos, newly elected President Van Buren called a special session of Congress. Fillmore set out for Washington filled with anger at a government whose policies he blamed for the current economic conditions.

Frustration and Opposition

On arriving in Washington, Fillmore was discouraged to find the city quite different from what he had left two years before. Although its physical appearance remained the same, the opulence and sense of gaiety had disappeared, destroyed by the economic depression and fear that gripped the nation.

Fillmore also was disappointed with President Van Buren's strategy for dealing with the crisis. Speaking to Congress, Van Buren outlined a two-pronged approach. He proposed to replace the system of state, or "pet," banks with a group of regional depositories owned and operated by the U.S. Treasury. This plan, known as the "independent" or "subtreasury" system, was designed to remove the federal government from the insecurities of the private banking system. President Van Buren's second proposal was to shore up the government's income by allowing the U.S. Treasury to default on promised payments of federal surplus funds to states—funds that were longer available because of the economic downturn.

Fillmore could see nothing but trouble in Van Buren's proposals. What Fillmore favored was a "free banking" system—not a national bank, or pet banks, or an independent Treasury, but rather banks untainted by politics. He urged Congress to:

> . . . purge [our banking system] of its corruptions and abuses, and strip it of its odious monopoly, and open the privilege of banking to all those who comply with such prescribed rules of the legislature as secure the bill-holder and public generally from fraud and imposition. I . . . hope to see the day when . . . the moral pestilence of political banks and banking shall be unknown.

But in spite of Fillmore's opposition and the opposition of other Whigs and a growing number of anti-Van Buren

Democrats, both of the President's measures passed in Congress. However, Fillmore's eloquent opposition to Van Buren's policies attracted the attention of prominent Whigs and others in the government.

The Antislavery Movement

In the fall of 1838, Fillmore was re-elected to his congressional seat without any difficulty. But in the meantime, a new movement was gathering strength — a movement that was to have a great influence on politics in the decades to come.

Four days after being nominated to run again for Congress, Fillmore found a questionnaire from the local antislavery society in his morning mail. It asked whether or not he favored abolishing slavery in all the states and in Washington, D.C. Although he answered "yes" to the questions, Millard refused to make any pledges that would tie his hands politically. For abolition of slavery was about to become the most volatile of all national political issues, and, as a shrewd politician, he wanted to avoid committing himself to one side or the other until he could clearly read the public sentiment on the issue.

The 1838 elections marked the Whigs' ascendance to national political power. Fed up with the depression and with the Democrats' approach to dealing with it, voters turned out in hordes to "vote the rascals out." Throughout the nation, in state and congressional elections, Whig candidates benefitted from the Democrats' collapse. The Whigs even gained a majority in the House of Representatives.

But even as they ascended to power, the Whigs were sowing the very seeds of their eventual political downfall. They badly misjudged the extent of public support behind the antislavery movement. Virtually ignoring the movement, they instead spent their time congratulating themselves and attributing their success to the widespread appeal of their astute economic policies.

RISING INFLUENCE

Upon entering his third term in Congress, Fillmore found he commanded increasing political influence. The Whigs were already preparing for the 1840 presidential election in which New York would play a prominent role. As western New York's most important Whig, Fillmore naturally would have much influence on the choice of candidate.

After much consideration and deliberation – and with as much resignation to political reality as enthusiasm – Fillmore finally threw his support behind William Henry Harrison. Confirming Fillmore's political instincts and judgment, Harrison received the presidential nomination on the third ballot at the Whig National Convention in December 1839.

Fire on the Floor

As yet another indication of his rising political influence, Fillmore was named to the House's Committee on Elections. From this post, he played an important role in a serious dispute between the Whigs and Democrats over some 1838 election results. Arguing the Whig position on the floor of Congress, he displayed a fire and tenacity that few knew he possessed. At one point, frustrated with the Speaker of the House's maneuvers to keep him from presenting his report on the election results, Fillmore exploded:

> I speak by right, and not by permission. I will never tamely . . . submit to yield a right . . . guaranteed by the Constitution. I would as willingly be the slave of one master as of a thousand.

In a fit of fury, the usually calm, dignified Millard Fillmore had lost his composure. Although censured by the Speaker, he gained new admiration from his colleagues. His tenacity in fighting for his party and his ability to stand up to a hostile House leadership pointed up his leadership qualities, and others were taking notice.

WHIG VICTORY

As the presidential election of 1840 neared, Fillmore put his increasing power to good use. Privately, he and his Whig colleagues on the Committee on Elections issued their report on the disputed election results of 1838 in a pamphlet and distributed it widely. Through Thomas Foote's editorial columns in the *Commercial Advertiser*, he savaged the Democrats and their tactics. As he told one colleague, it was all part of his effort to "keep the steam up" to ensure Whig success in the vital election year of 1840.

The election results of that year surpassed Fillmore's wildest hopes. The Whigs swept the nation, winning 12 governorships, majorities in both Houses of Congress, and, for William Henry Harrison, the presidency. As expected, Fillmore himself won his congressional seat with ease, and western New York solidified its position as a Whig stronghold. For the first time in his 12-year political career, Fillmore belonged to the nation's ruling elite.

Chapter 4

In the National Arena

In his new position of power, Congressman Fillmore would now have greater influence on national economic policy and political events. He wasted little time exercising this influence.

The Whigs inherited a gloomy economic situation from the Democrats in 1840. The depression had worsened, and the federal government was deep in debt. Desperate merchants, manufacturers, bankers, and investors turned to the incoming Whigs for help.

INTERNAL DISPUTES

But before the politicians in Washington could help their favored constituents, they had to settle their own internal disputes. For despite their recent victories, the Whig leadership was in serious disarray. President Harrison was seen only as a vote-getter and a figurehead, not as a strong leader. Seeing his chance to capture a position of party leadership, Henry Clay proposed a program of economic relief and called for a special session of Congress to enact it immediately into law. Through this strategy, Clay hoped to promote himself as the party's true head.

But Daniel Webster, whom President Harrison had chosen as secretary of state to lead his Cabinet, had his own plans for capturing the Whig leadership. Webster hoped that by controlling the Harrison administration through his position in the Cabinet, he would be able to use the party for his own purposes.

As Clay and Webster strove to outmaneuver each other, the divisions among the Whigs deepened. Fillmore, determined to keep Clay from capturing the party leadership, threw his support behind Webster and hoped to become Speaker of the House of Representatives. When Clay finally convinced President Harrison to call the special session of Congress, Fillmore circulated among the incoming congressmen, trying to stir up support for the speakership. However, when Clay's candidate for the same position, Representative John White of Tennessee, was in the lead after several ballots, Fillmore graciously withdrew from the running. Thus, Clay drew even with Webster in the struggle for Whig leadership.

Tragedy Strikes

But just as the Whigs seemed about to reach an uneasy harmony among themselves and finally begin to direct their attentions toward the nation's problems, tragedy struck. President Harrison contracted pneumonia and died on April 4, 1841, just a month after his inauguration.

Harrison's successor, Virginia aristocrat John Tyler, vehemently opposed a national bank and protective tariffs (taxes on imported goods) and ardently favored states' rights and slavery. Tyler's beliefs were in direct opposition to Clay's proposed economic recovery program, which rested on a new national bank, a new uniform national currency, distribution to the states of revenue from the sale of public lands, a national bankruptcy law, and a strong protective tariff.

Disharmony Increases

At first Clay anticipated no problems in gaining Tyler's support for his proposals. But time and again, a petulant (peevish) Tyler vetoed Whig-sponsored bills that had been passed by Congress. As the rupture between Tyler and Clay became more bitter, party harmony dissolved even further.

Dismayed by President Tyler's vetoes, Clay resolved to gain power through other means. He conspired with certain influential Whigs in an attempt to discredit Tyler by organizing a mass resignation of Tyler's Cabinet. Although he generally opposed Clay's policies and disapproved of his presidential ambitions, Fillmore felt he had little choice but to join in. Not to go along with Clay at this point would split the Whigs – particularly in New York – perhaps to a fatal degree.

Repudiating the President

So, as Congress adjourned their special session, a group of 50 prominent Whigs issued a proclamation to the people of the United States. In it, they repudiated President Tyler and his policies and declared that the alliance between Tyler and the Whigs was now severed. From that point on, Tyler was a President without a party. Henry Clay became the new national Whig leader.

With their internal problems solved at least momentarily, the Whigs turned their attention to the nation's pressing economic problems. To help spearhead their economic reform program, they named Millard Fillmore as chairman of the House Ways and Means Committee.

INTO THE BREACH

Although he had lost his bid to become Speaker of the House, Fillmore did not lose his chance to affect the political destiny of the nation. By tradition, the runner-up in the speaker-

Through skillful political maneuvering, fiery and eloquent Henry Clay ascended to the leadership of the national Whig Party by 1842. (Library of Congress.)

ship race was given the chairmanship of the powerful House Ways and Means Committee. In 1841, critical economic times made this chairmanship doubly important. More than three-quarters of the Whig economic recovery program would be in his hands. Only 15 years earlier, young Fillmore was counting his pennies and struggling to survive as a lawyer's apprentice. Now, at the age of 41, he would be directing the finances of a nation.

Fillmore accepted the post eagerly. From it, he could not only espouse the economic and political ideas he held dear, but also put those ideas into practice. In economic policy, Fillmore fancied himself a pragmatist (one who takes a practical approach to problems) rather than an idealist. He believed that the path to economic recovery lay in a program that encouraged and protected American industry and commerce—a program that, in his view, depended on strong protective tariffs that discouraged importation of foreign goods to compete with American products.

The Tariff Act of 1842

Fillmore wasted no time in translating his beliefs into action. He began by throwing his support behind the National Bankruptcy Act of 1841. This act gave heavily indebted businessmen the opportunity to declare bankruptcy and thus "wipe the slate clean" so they could start over in new business ventures.

With even more enthusiasm—if with little of Henry Clay's fire and flamboyance—Fillmore steered his tariff proposal through Congress. After much political wrangling between Congress and President Tyler, in June Tyler signed into law the Tariff Act of 1842.

This act provided several means for discouraging imports, including higher overall tariff rates, fixing of rates based on the value of the goods in the United States rather than in their country of origin, and payment of tariffs immediately on importation of goods, with no grace period.

Praise for the Chairman

These new policies had an almost immediate effect. Buoyed by an upsurge in manufacturing, particularly in the northeastern states, the depression began to lift. Regardless of whether the Tariff Act of 1842 was responsible for the return of prosperity, the Whigs were quick to claim the credit. And from every quarter of the industrial and commercial community came acclaim for the young chairman of the Ways and Means Committee who had so well represented their interests.

Not only Fillmore's policies but also the way in which he implemented them drew high praise. Beneath his placid, dignified exterior Millard had revealed a reservoir of untapped strength. Often in the midst of a stormy session, he had risen and in a commanding manner stilled the uproar. To many, he showed evidence of true leadership ability. He was always dignified, cool, self-possessed, clear, and indefatiguable (untiring); now and then he even demonstrated eloquence. "Fillmore," one of his admirers remarked, "is a great man; but it takes strong pressure to make him show his highest powers."

Few of these admirers would have believed Millard then, had he told them of his plans. For at this peak in his career, when the prospect of even greater success lay before him, Fillmore had decided to retire from Congress.

Chapter 5

On the Local Stage

Throughout the 18 months the Whigs had held national power, they had been steadily losing support at the local level. In New York, the situation was particularly troublesome. Weakened by internal disputes surrounding Governor Seward and his party adversaries, and challenged by the new American Republican Party (or the "Native Americans" as they were popularly known) and the resurgent Liberty Party (the party of New York's antislavery activists), the foundations of New York's Whig Party were crumbling.

In June 1842, troubled by these developments and feeling that he could accomplish little more in Congress than he had already been able to do, Fillmore decided to decline his renomination to Congress. Instead, he would return to Buffalo to the "quiet enjoyment of my own family and fireside."

AN ACTIVE RETIREMENT

With Fillmore back in Buffalo, his law practice prospered. Although he seemed content to spend the next few years busy with his practice, enjoying the esteem of his fellow Buffalonians, and laying the foundation for an income that would enable him and his family to live comfortably, his hand remained on the controls of the Whig Party in western New York. He eagerly devoured the latest political news from Albany and Washington.

The national Whig Party had not forgotten him. In the summer of 1843, former President John Quincy Adams, to many the "grand old man" of the Whigs, visited Buffalo to speak. Fillmore was given the privilege of extending the city's official welcome. Impressed by Fillmore's introduction, Adams remarked in his speech:

> I cannot forbear to express here my regret at [Fillmore's] retirement in this present emergency from the councils of his nation. There, or elsewhere, I hope and trust he will soon return, for whether to the nation or to the state, no service can be or ever will be rendered by a more able or a more faithful public servant.

Plans for a Return

Little did Adams know that he would not have long to wait. For as Adams spoke, Fillmore was already making plans to return to Washington. Even before he left Congress in 1842, several influential Whigs had brought up the idea of nominating him for Vice-President for the election of 1844. At first, Fillmore did nothing to promote his candidacy, although he certainly was flattered by the consideration. But by the spring of 1843, he was inextricably entangled in a web of behind-the-scenes moves to gain the nomination.

Except for politicians, few in the nation concerned themselves with vice-presidential candidacies. Attention was focused almost totally on the presidential contest. By the fall of 1843, even before the national convention was held in Baltimore, Henry Clay was assured of the Whig presidential nomination. Throughout this time, Fillmore's candidacy for the vice-presidential nomination was progressing well. He aimed his efforts at winning the pledge of New York's delegates to the national convention. At the convention, with his state's large block of votes behind him and his record on the tariff bill and other economic issues to recommend him, he hoped for victory. But securing the support of New York's delegation proved to be no easy task.

Weed's Scheme

By this time, Thurlow Weed's grip on the New York Whigs had loosened considerably. Spurred by dissatisfaction with Weed-backed Governor William Seward, whose administration was mired in financial woes, a powerful anti-Weed faction had developed, centered in New York City. In 1843 this group formally split with Weed by naming their own candidate, John A. Collier, for the governorship of New York. Their second choice was Luther Bradish. If both of these men failed, the anti-Weed faction was willing to settle on Millard Fillmore. Weed rejected all three men, and offered Willis Hall as his candidate. For Seward, Weed had other plans — to make him the Whig vice-presidential candidate for the 1844 election.

Learning of Weed's plan, Fillmore retaliated by meeting with Collier and offering him a deal. In return for Collier's support for his vice-presidential candidacy at the Baltimore convention, Fillmore promised to throw his weight behind Collier for the New York governorship.

Whig members foresaw a major struggle developing between Fillmore and Seward. But Seward, painfully aware of the hostility he and Weed had caused in party ranks, surprised Weed by withdrawing his name from consideration for the vice-presidential nomination. Unable to change Seward's mind, Weed then changed his own plans. He arranged a meeting with Fillmore, Seward, and Willis Hall. At the meeting, the four men agreed that Seward would not run for any office, that Seward and Weed would support Fillmore for Vice-President, and that Fillmore, if he failed to win the nomination in Baltimore, would not become a candidate for governor against Hall.

Desperate Solutions

All might have gone well except for an unforeseen event. Just as these arrangements were being finalized, Willis Hall was struck with a serious illness that made him unable to continue as a candidate for governor. Weed's predicament was obvious; now the anti-Weed faction's candidate, either Collier or Bradish, was in a favorable position to capture the Whig nomination for governor of New York.

Desperate, Weed searched for a solution to his predicament. More concerned with his own political fortunes than with Fillmore's destiny, he began a campaign to defeat Fillmore's vice-presidential candidacy. By doing so, he hoped to leave Fillmore no alternative but to run for governor.

Tirelessly, Weed promoted Fillmore as the only man who could save New York State for the Whigs. Weed appealed to the state party to reject Fillmore for Vice-President and to nominate him for governor. At first, Millard was unaware of Weed's motives and naturally was flattered by Weed's seeming confidence in his abilities. But soon Weed made a fatal mistake.

Fillmore learned that Weed had revived Seward's nomination for Vice-President (although Seward himself still was refusing to participate). Stung by yet another incidence of Weed's political skullduggery, Fillmore vowed not to cooperate with his scheme. As he confided to his friend, Francis Granger:

> I receive letters from my friends in various parts of the state stating that Governor Seward's most intimate friends are "killing me with kindness." It is said they have discovered that it is indispensable that my name should be used for the office of governor, and that it would be unjust to me and ruinous to the Whig party in the state, if I am nominated for the office of Vice-President. I need not say to you that I have no desire to run for governor . . . I am not willing to be treacherously killed by this pretended kindness . . . Do not suppose for a moment that I think they desire my nomination for governor.

A Sense of Foreboding

Under the circumstances, Fillmore went to the Whig convention in Baltimore with a sense of foreboding about the fate of his vice-presidential candidacy. His fears proved well-founded. Although New York's delegation arrived in Baltimore pledged to Henry Clay for the presidential nomination, they had not yet committed themselves to a vice-presidential candidate. Weed himself traveled to Baltimore, spreading the word among the delegates from other states that the New York Whigs would be glad to see Fillmore passed by, since they needed him to run for governor.

Weed's scheme worked. On the third ballot, the convention gave the vice-presidential nomination to Theodore Frelinghuysen of New Jersey. Fillmore was crushed, feeling that his work of the past two years had been for nothing.

Putting Up a Front

Although stung by failure, Fillmore tried hard to put up a good front for the sake of the party. On his way home from Baltimore, he met Frelinghuysen and Collier at a Whig rally in New York City. There, all three men appeared on the platform, smiling in an outward show of party unity. But Fillmore could not totally conceal his feelings. Even the offer of the New York City Whig leaders to dismiss Collier and join with Weed in making Millard the unanimous Whig nominee for governor could not dispel his deep disappointment. Citing his previous commitment to Collier and his distrust of Weed, he quickly declined the offer.

But the growing antislavery movement in New York began to pressure Fillmore into changing his mind. In 1844, the question of whether or not to annex Texas into the Union was an important national issue that raised the explosive possibility of the expansion of slavery. Even before the Whig National Convention, Henry Clay had gone on record against the annexation of Texas. The Democrats, on the other hand, supported annexation—which earned them support in the West and the South. Whigs in these regions began to pressure Clay. Feeling his popularity in danger of ebbing, Clay quickly modified his position, stating that he wished to see Texas added to the Union "upon just and fair terms" and that "the subject of slavery ought not to affect the question one way or the other."

Antislavery Support

Clay's new stand had immediate political repercussions in New York. The antislavery voters who had remained with the Whigs and who would have been willing to vote for Clay on a no-annexation platform now shifted their support to James G. Birney, nominee of the fledgling Liberty Party. Inadvertently, Fillmore now found himself in a position to aid the national ticket. Over the past decade, he had gained a good reputation among the abolitionists (antislavery adherents). Although he did not have the abolitionists' zeal, he did oppose slavery. More through accident than design, Fillmore rose high on the abolitionists' list of acceptable officeholders.

While the antislavery movement began to stir ominously against the Whigs, Weed increased his pressure on Fillmore to run for governor. Others joined in Weed's effort. But Fillmore continued to resist. Finally understanding the reason for Fillmore's reluctance, Weed redirected his efforts toward persuading John Collier to withdraw from consideration and thus clear the way for Fillmore.

Running for Governor

Weed began putting intense pressure on Collier, so much so that Collier soon felt obliged to withdraw. To the end, Fillmore insisted that he did not seek the office. But finally, he felt he had to bow to the will of the people and accept the nomination. When informed that he had won the nomination, he accepted somewhat less than enthusiastically: "So I am in for it and there is no escape." For his running mate as lieutenant-governor, the state convention chose Samuel J. Wilkins, a skilled lawyer and politician who had joined the Whig Party in its Antimason days.

To run against Fillmore, the Democrats nominated Senator Silas Wright of New York. The campaign was tough and bitter. The Whigs were besieged not only by the Democrats but also by the Liberty Party and the American Republicans, or "Nativists," whom the Democrats courted and somewhat successfully turned against the Whig cause. Fillmore covered the state, delivering speech after speech espousing the Whig positions on Texas, abolition, "nativism," and the economy. But as the election neared, a feeling of gloom pervaded the Whigs, who felt the battle turning against them. This feeling proved prophetic, as the entire Whig ticket went down in defeat.

In one of the most closely contested presidential elections ever, Henry Clay narrowly lost to Democratic candidate James K. Polk. In the New York governor's race, Fillmore polled 231,057 votes to Silas Wright's 241,090.

A NEW DIRECTION

"All is gone but honor," Fillmore lamented when his defeat was certain. Not wasting much time brooding over the election results—he felt that Weed and Seward had led him into a trap and that his defeat was inevitable—Millard retired once again to his law practice in Buffalo. He enjoyed living in Buffalo and enjoyed his family. Often he would take time off from his practice to be with his wife and children. When Powers turned 16, Fillmore took him into the law office as a student. Mary Abigail was in her early teens and deeply involved in music lessons.

At home, Fillmore strove to create the same atmosphere of gentility and dignity for which he was noted in public life. His wife, Abigail, was the envy of the wives in the Fillmores' circle of friends as her husband showered her with all the affection, respect, and courtesy that most other men reserved for guests.

In these pleasant surroundings, Fillmore tried to bury himself in a busy professional and home life. Before long, however, the routine uneventfulness of his days began to wear thin, and he yearned for a return to public life. Although he served as chancellor at the University of Buffalo, which he had helped found, this hardly satisfied his urge to be back in the thick of public affairs, nor did his involvement in a movement to secure federal funds to expand Buffalo's harbor and canal system. The frequent visits of politicians and statesmen only reminded Fillmore of his days as a respected and influential congressman, making retirement even more unbearable.

"Boss" Fillmore

As the midterm elections of 1846 approached, Fillmore decided that if he could not serve in public office, he could use his still-considerable influence to help elect candidates of his choice. He set about to promote Whig unity in western New York. Although he had no ambition to be a political "boss" like Thurlow Weed, Fillmore saw that his position could be very valuable to party harmony. He began on the local level by persuading his law partner, Solomon G. Haven, to run for mayor of Buffalo. When Haven won, Fillmore was encouraged to form a committee to back the campaign of Nathan K. Hall, a former partner, for Congress. Hall's easy nomination showed how well Fillmore had smoothed the way.

Over the next several months, Fillmore solidified his position in the party. In the process, he began to erode Weed's influence, which had been steadily declining anyway since the disastrous election of 1844. Whigs in various parts of New York, particularly in New York City, were actively trying to dethrone "Dictator Weed," as some took to calling him. At the state Whig convention in 1846, Fillmore-backed John Young won the gubernatorial nomination over Weed's man, Ira Harris. Young's subsequent victory in the 1846 election returned the Whigs to power in New York and further solidified Fillmore's position—and reduced Weed's power.

Back in the Running

After Young's election as governor, Whigs set their sights on filling other important state offices that were up for election in 1847. The most significant of these was the state comptrollership. In many ways this office was the most important one in the state, as the man in the position had far more direct control over the state's finances than any other officeholder—including the governor. The Whigs knew they needed a strong candidate for the post to succeed against the incumbent (currently serving), Democrat Azariah C. Flagg.

Recognizing what he had done for the party over the past year and examining his previous record, the Whigs chose Fillmore. When his friends approached him about the nomination, Fillmore accepted eagerly. He had already decided once and for all to forego the pleasures of "retirement" for the excitement of the political arena. Although he would have preferred the office of U.S. senator to state comptroller, he was ready to assume any office if it furthered the cause he held dear—Whig victory.

The Comptrollership

The results of the election of 1847 confirmed Fillmore's confidence in his abilities and power. He won by the largest margin—over 30,000 votes—that any Whig had ever received for a state office. Shortly after his election, Fillmore visited Albany to arrange for apartments for himself and his family and to inspect the comptroller's office. The warm reception that he received convinced him that from now on, his life would not be spent in the quiet practice of law. Rather, it would be in the spotlight of the political stage, where he was to become a prominent actor.

Once settled in office, Fillmore carried out the duties of comptroller in the manner that his admirers expected. Under his guidance, canal and harbor improvements leaped ahead. He also introduced a new currency system that Congress adopted as part of the National Banking Act 16 years later. But while the routine of his office occupied most of Fillmore's time, his attention remained fixed on the national political scene, where he now knew his destiny lay.

Chapter 6

The Road to the White House

Had Fillmore and the other Whig leaders been able to foretell the future in 1847, they would have seen a party fated to wither and die within the next eight years. But with all of their combined wisdom, none of the party chiefs had an inkling of the catastrophe to come. Instead, they allowed the pressures of the moment and the need to win local elections to blind them to the larger issues that would soon swamp the party. Hungry for success, northern Whigs—the party's stronghold—began experimenting with the national issue of slavery in local elections. Unfortunately, this experimentation was to prove fatal to the party and, ultimately, to the nation's unity.

SEEDS OF DISUNITY

Those same Whig leaders who had initially shunned the question of abolition like a disease now embraced it as a national party issue. In Massachusetts, John Quincy Adams and

Charles Sumner created the so-called "Conscience Whigs," stridently antislavery and popular among rural voters. Those who refused to follow their lead were branded as defenders of slavery and derided as "Cotton Whigs" (because many large slaveholders were southern cotton growers). All over the North, this schism split the party.

The Wilmot Proviso

While the Whigs were occupied with their internal struggles, the Wilmot Proviso added another issue to the coming election campaign of 1848. Everyone knew that at the end of the Mexican War the United States would acquire the territory west of Texas, including California. The big question was: Should this territory be free or slave?

Democratic Representative David Wilmot of Pennsylvania tried to persuade Congress to pledge in advance to prohibit slavery in any land that might be acquired from Mexico. The House of Representatives passed the measure in 1846, but the Senate declined to vote on it. Over the next few years, antislavery leaders seized on the Wilmot Proviso as a statement of their guiding principle and a test of a politician's committment to their cause.

A Complicated Dilemma

The southern Whigs, meanwhile, looked on the developments in the North with dismay. After all, they represented the region's large slaveholders, but their northern colleagues were becoming increasingly caught up in the new antislavery furor sweeping the nation. Southern Whig leaders, who had been steadily losing influence since the 1842 election, now faced a complicated dilemma—how to regain influence within the party and at the same time stem the abolitionist tide. They hastily agreed to a simple strategy: win the presidential election of 1848 with a southern candidate that the northern Whigs could accept.

For their candidate, the southern Whigs chose General Zachary Taylor, who was then receiving popular acclaim for leading the U.S. Army to victory after victory in the Mexican War. Recognizing the appeal of a war hero to voters—remembering Generals Washington, Jackson, and Harrison—a group of predominantly southern Whigs known as the "Young Indians" convinced Taylor to run.

Biding Time

While the Taylor campaign unfolded in the South, Fillmore took stock of his own position. He was thriving in the New York state comptrollership, displaying, again, as a colleague put it, "the peculiar faculty of adapting himself to every position in which he served." But beyond his administrative talents, he was now developing a new confidence in his political skill and in his political destiny.

Fillmore's five-year absence from office (1842-1847)—years enriched by his successful law practice—had given him a new perspective on politics. And his successful maneuvers against Thurlow Weed in the 1846 campaign had emboldened him. From the moment he took over the state comptrollership, Fillmore acted as if a greater destiny awaited him.

Meanwhile, Weed was fuming in his newspaper office in Albany. His influence within the party was at a new low, and he could not seem to find a clear course back to power.

What was worse, the party's most promising candidate seemed under the control of the southern wing of the party. (Weed had been among the northern Whigs who cautiously embraced antislavery as a way out of his problems.)

Fillmore, too, might have been wary of the southerners. After all, they were the ones responsible for the repeal of the Tariff Act of 1842, his crowning achievement thus far. But he felt no concern. Instead, the rise of a strong southern candidate left him feeling content and confident of the Whigs recapturing the presidency.

Weed's Secret Plan

Weed, on the other hand, was intent on recovering his power. To this end, he identified one ultimate goal: eliminating the southern faction of the Whig Party. Like others who had waged a hate campaign against the South, Weed was deeply disturbed about Taylor's growing strength. To offset it, he devised a strategy in which he alternately endorsed Clay, Harrison, and a changing compromise candidate.

Weed also attempted to mend his personal and political relationship with Fillmore. Early in 1848, he called on Fillmore to talk about presidential politics. With his legendary cunning, he persuaded Fillmore to cooperate with his strategy. As Weed put it, no matter who was nominated at the national convention, New York Whigs would be on the winning side. "I will go along with Weed in this," Fillmore wrote to his former law partner, Solomon G. Haven, "as long as it is not harmful to the best interest of the party. But we must win the national election."

But, as usual, Weed was not being totally honest with Fillmore. He did not share with Millard one part of his scheme — secretly promoting William Seward as a dark-horse presidential candidate.

Another Weed Plan

In the meantime, Taylor's managers selected Abbott Lawrence as Taylor's vice-presidential running mate. Lawrence, a textile manufacturer and a trader, was one of the nation's wealthiest men. He was identified as a "Cotton Whig," not prone to antislavery pronouncements. Repelled by Lawrence's association with slaveholders, the "Conscience Whigs" were outraged.

Fillmore and Weed also gave thought to the vice-presidential candidate. Again, Weed had a plan. By endorsing Lawrence, he hoped to gain favor with Taylor and insinuate (slyly introduce) himself into the Taylor camp, which might be useful in the future.

Fillmore, however, viewed the situation differently. Even though certain prominent Whigs who had supported him in his bid for the 1844 vice-presidential nomination were again floating his name, Fillmore had his eyes on the party's success rather than on his own personal gain. Thus, he made no move to promote his own candidacy. Instead, in the interest of party harmony, he joined with Weed in supporting Lawrence. Despite all that had happened between them, Fillmore still believed that the Whig Party needed Weed, and acted accordingly.

THE CAMPAIGN OF 1848

In the spring of 1848, Whigs fought an exciting and bitter battle among themselves. On one side stood the southern Whigs, who, with scattered northern and western Whigs, were aligned with Taylor. On the other side were most of the northern

Whigs, split among several hopefuls — foremost among them being Henry Clay. Some northerners, notably the "Conscience Whigs," were strongly and sincerely antislavery. Most others, however, were more concerned with the economic implications of a southern- and western-dominated, agriculturally based Whig Party.

Further complicating matters was a new northern political party, the Free Soil Party, which threatened to steal some support from the northern Whigs. The Free Soilers appealed to antislavery voters by advocating the prohibition of slavery in new territories. They also appealed to agriculture voters by calling for free homesteads in the western lands. Seeing an opportunity to weaken their northern opponents, southern Whigs encouraged the Free Soilers. Several southern leaders even called for a union with the Free Soilers against the northern Whigs.

A Heated Convention

By the time the Whig National Convention assembled in June 1848, General Zachary Taylor's nomination was almost assured. Through several ballots, the Clay faction and other northerners resisted, afraid that the southern proslavery position would frighten off voters in the November election. But on the fourth ballot, Taylor was nominated in a stampede of emotion.

The reaction from the northerners was immediate and bitter. Slave-hating Charles Allen of Massachusetts leaped to the podium and, choking with rage, shouted his opposition to Taylor. "The free states will not submit," he sputtered. "By this nomination, the party is dissolved." The assembly exploded in a deafening chorus of cheers, boos, and hisses.

After many minutes, order was finally restored, and John A. Collier seized the floor. In a conciliatory speech, the most prominent member of the New York delegation magnanimously pledged New York's support of Taylor. Collier then announced that he had a peace offering to suggest. It was an offering which, if the Taylor supporters accepted it, would reconcile the supporters of all the defeated candidates and prevent a fatal split in the party. To the astonishment of the audience, Collier named Millard Fillmore for Vice-President.

Fillmore's Candidacy

Collier's move was timed perfectly. As they overcame their astonishment, the assembly rushed to nominate Fillmore. Supporters of Abbott Lawrence tried to stem the tide, but could not. On the second ballot, the convention nominated Millard Fillmore as the Whig vice-presidential candidate for 1848.

In many respects, Fillmore's easy victory came for the wrong reasons. Many at the convention wrongly assumed that because he was nominated by Collier, a pro-Clay delegate and aligned with the mostly pro-Clay New York Whigs, that Fillmore himself was a Clay supporter. But in fact, Fillmore had never been and was not now behind Clay.

Soon after the campaign began, Fillmore set about demonstrating that he was neither behind Clay nor behind the antislavery movement (at least in the sense that he intended to do anything about abolishing or limiting slavery). In a speech to some southern Whig leaders, he clearly and concisely outlined his stance on the issue. He had always . . .

> . . . regarded slavery as an evil, but one with which the national government had nothing to do. That by the Constitution of the United States the whole power over that question

The national Whig Party ticket for the election of 1848 included Zachary Taylor for President and a compromise candidate, Millard Fillmore, for Vice-President. (Library of Congress.)

was vested in the several states where the institution was toler-
ated. If they regarded it as a blessing, they had a constitu-
tional right to enjoy it; and if they regarded it as an evil, they
had the power and knew best how to apply the remedy. I did
not conceive that Congress had power over it, or was in any
way responsible for its continuance over the several states
where it existed.

In all his public proclamations about slavery, never once
did Fillmore mention anything about slavery in the western
territories or the federal government's responsibility for it.
He skillfully walked a political tightrope on the issue, keeping his appeal as broad as possible.

An Old Adversary

But as serious as the slavery issue was to Fillmore in the
South, his greatest challenge came from an old adversary in
the North—Thurlow Weed. Clay supporters were still seeth-
ing over their defeat at the convention, and talk of running
Clay as an independent presidential candidate grew more seri-
ous. In an effort to persuade the state Whig Party to abandon
Taylor in favor of Clay, Weed called for a mass meeting of
New York Whigs.

On hearing of Weed's plan, Fillmore became worried.
Whatever he thought of Taylor, Fillmore's future—and the future of the entire Whig Party—was tied to Taylor's candidacy.
In a heated visit to Weed's office, Fillmore demanded that
Weed call off the mass meeting. After a day and an evening
of discussion and negotiation, the two men reached an agreement. First, the meeting would be postponed for several days,
then held for a different purpose. Second, the two would send
a letter to Taylor asking that he try to mend party differences.

Saving Party Unity

As agreed, two days later the mass meeting was convened at the capitol in Albany. Its whole purpose, however, had been turned on its end. Instead of a forum for expressing dissatisfaction with Taylor, it became a platform for denouncing Taylor's detractors. Guided by Fillmore, Weed, and John A. Collier, the party adopted a resolution wholeheartedly supporting Taylor, and the meeting adjourned with cheers for Taylor and Fillmore.

Fillmore's successful joust with Weed had saved Whig Party unity in New York. This proved critical when election returns were tabulated in November. The margin was narrow, and the Taylor-Fillmore victory hinged on the New York vote. For his role, Fillmore should have earned the gratitude of Taylor and the entire party. But instead of boasting of his prowess and seeking that gratitude, Fillmore was content to enjoy his and the party's success and await what he was sure would be a rosy future. Flushed with victory, he did not anticipate Weed's next move.

BETRAYED!

Fillmore thoroughly enjoyed the four months between the election and his inauguration. Wherever he went, he radiated charm and goodwill, his pink, rotund face glowing with good humor. The week after winning the election, he traveled from Albany to New York City for a gala Whig celebration. As Seward reported to Weed, with more than a trace of bitterness, "The people were full of demonstrations of affection to the Vice-President."

Fillmore had attained a position of great prestige, and possibly of great influence, too, President Taylor, aware of the great burdens that lay before him, had remarked, "I wish Mr. Fillmore would take all of the business into his own hands." So sure was Fillmore of his position that he remained in Albany until the eve of the inauguration to make sure all the affairs of the comptroller's office were in order. But unfortunately, he was letting his confidence and good spirits cloud his political judgment.

A Weedy Plot

During the months between election and inauguration, Weed pondered his latest predicament. For the past four years, Whig leaders had succeeded in limiting his power within the party. Repeatedly, Fillmore had joined with Weed's enemies, and now Fillmore was fast becoming, in Weed's mind, "the New York leader in the general counsel of the Whigs of the Union." For the next four (or perhaps eight) years, Weed and Seward faced the unpleasant prospect of opposing Fillmore.

Weed could see only one way out of his predicament— he had to curtail Fillmore's growing power. To do so, he needed someone to counterbalance Fillmore in Washington. He was in luck. John A. Dix, a U.S. senator from New York, was about to retire, and Weed began planning for Seward's election to the post. His plan met with much opposition from New York Whigs, many of whom favored John A. Collier for the Senate position. Between November 1848 and January 1849, when the state legislature was to meet to select the new senator, Weed became bolder. At a point when Collier seemed to have secured the post, Weed turned to his intended (and unwary) victim—Fillmore—for help.

Good Faith; Bad Judgment

The cunning Weed made his move when Fillmore's guard was down. Seemingly innocently, Weed asked Fillmore for his support for Seward in the coming legislative caucus (meeting of party members). In return, Weed promised to cooperate with Fillmore in every way for joint control of the state.

Fillmore had two reasons for cooperating with Weed. First, it was wise politics for him to secure such an arrangement on the verge of his promotion to the national arena. Second, it would help strengthen the Whig Party. In good faith — although in bad judgment — he accepted Weed's offer. Bolstered by Fillmore's support, Seward won the senate seat.

Just before leaving for Washington in late February 1849, Fillmore dined with Weed and Seward in Albany. They renewed their pledges of cooperation and arranged some details. As Weed recorded in his autobiography, "The Vice-President and Senator were to consult from time to time, as should become necessary, and agree upon the important appointments to be made in our state." However, Weed's private directions to Seward were different, centering around two tasks: to destroy Fillmore's possible control of the federal patronage for New York, and to sway President Taylor away from the southern Whig influence.

THE INAUGURATION

Inauguration day — Monday, March 5, 1849 — dawned cold and cloudy, with a hint of snow in the air. As usual, Fillmore arose early, even though the official carriage that would carry him to the Capitol for the ceremony would not be arriving until

*The Willard House, at 14th Street and Pennsylvania Avenue in
Washington, D.C., was Fillmore's residence and base of opera-
tions when he was a congressman and, later, Vice-President.*
(National Archives.)

11 o'clock. He was staying at the Willard House, his base of
operations when he had been a congressman.

The week before, when he had arrived in Washington,
Fillmore had met President-elect Taylor at the Willard—their
first meeting ever. They had passed some time in pleasant
conversation, but spoke little of the political situation and of
any plans for the upcoming administration. Although Taylor
was putting together his Cabinet, never once did he call on
his running mate—whose knowledge went back 20 years—
for advice. At the time, Fillmore felt no concern about this
oversight.

Inauguration day was more Taylor's triumph than Fillmore's, of course. But as the Vice-President-elect's carriage moved along Pennsylvania Avenue to the Capitol, the crowds cheered. Fillmore's broad, cheerful face reflected the spirit of the day. And as he removed his hat from time to time, his long white hair blowing in the breeze, he looked a picture of dignity, competence, and geniality.

A Packed Gallery

Fillmore's own inauguration ceremony, unlike the President's, took place in the Senate chamber. Flanked by a senatorial honor committee, he entered the room shortly before noon. The room was filled with all sorts of celebrities and statesmen. The tiny visitors' gallery was so packed that three women fainted before the ceremony started.

In a deep, confident voice, Fillmore repeated the oath of office given by the Chief Justice of the Supreme Court. Then he turned to the assembled senators and addressed them briefly. He expressed his faith in America's "capacity for self-government," and, peering into the future, he hoped that this capacity would be sustained, even in times of extreme crisis, so that "the glorious Union may endure forever." The assemblage listened politely, then adjourned. Noisily and cheerfully, they all moved outside to the main steps of the Capitol for the presidential inauguration, the main event of the day.

A Night of Partying

That evening, Fillmore and President Taylor drove through a snowstorm to three inaugural balls. The presidential party first stopped at Carusi's Saloon, then at Jackson Hall, and finally made their way to the formal ball at City Hall. Here, between four and five thousand people danced and toasted the new administration into power. Before dawn, when the festivities finally ended, Vice-President Fillmore returned to his rooms at the Willard, tired and a bit concerned. Although he had spent the entire evening with President Taylor, he felt no closer to him now than he had a week before, when they first met.

Secret Actions

In the meantime, newly appointed Senator William Seward of New York was putting Thurlow Weed's secret plan into action. Seward spent the weeks before the inauguration meeting with President-elect Taylor's confirmed and rumored Cabinet officers. Slowly, an alliance began to form between the Taylor administration and the Weed "machine." This alliance was strengthened by other political developments.

In a shrewd move, President Taylor's team had positioned themselves on both sides of the Wilmot Proviso issue. They planned to divide the new territory acquired from Mexico into states and admit them into the Union. These new states would then decide for themselves whether to be free or slave, thus saving the administration from having to make a politically troublesome decision on slavery in the territory. At the same time, they would be achieving the objective of the Wilmot Proviso without actually having to endorse it.

To help strengthen their team, President Taylor's advisors linked up with Seward and Weed. Taylor was not aware of the nature of this alliance at first (and possibly never). In secret, an agreement was set. In return for Seward's support of the Taylor plan in Congress, Weed would be given control of the political patronage that the Taylor team controlled in New York. To avoid a public breach between Taylor's advisors and Vice-President Fillmore—who knew nothing of these dealings—it was decided that the administration would give the public the impression that it recognized the Albany agreement between Fillmore and Weed, in which the two men were to share control of the state's patronage.

Weed's Manipulations

By the time Fillmore discovered Weed's trickery, it was too late. Weed had already arranged to fill several important positions in New York without consulting Fillmore. When Fillmore appealed to the President, Taylor refused to intervene until he talked to his advisors—the very same team that was involved secretly with Weed!

Deciding that he could not entrust such sensitive manipulations to Seward, Weed traveled to Washington himself. There, he met with President Taylor and convinced the President that the problem in New York was merely a personal conflict between Fillmore and Seward. After Weed also convinced the President that he had nothing but the party's best interests in mind, he persuaded Taylor to place control of New York patronage in the hands of newly elected Governor Hamilton Fish, whom all agreed was unbiased. Whether or not aware that Fish was Weed's tool, President Taylor was delighted with the solution, which seemed to promise a return to party harmony.

Open Attack

Putting patronage in the hands of Governor Fish assured supremacy in New York for Weed and Seward. With his scheme now exposed, Weed opened a direct attack on

Fillmore. All over the state, he arranged for his followers to gain patronage positions over Fillmore's choices. He conducted a blistering editorial campaign in his Albany newspaper, belittling Fillmore's authority. "We could put up a cow against a Fillmore nominee and defeat him," crowed one editorial. Many party members deserted Fillmore and aligned themselves with Weed, and Fillmore's popularity plummetted.

By mid-1849, Fillmore's situation had become desperate. In the past year, Weed had regained much of the political power he had lost over the previous four years and was now using this power to try and destroy the Vice-President. Fillmore's generous and trusting nature had led him to the edge of political destruction, and Weed was showing no mercy.

The Vice-President Fights Back

But Fillmore was not about to give up. In the summer of 1849 he began to gather around him an active group of men who shared his ideals and goals. This group of "young, zealous, active Whigs" was dedicated to restoring the balance in the New York party that Weed had destroyed. The men raised over $10,000 to start a new newspaper, the *Register*, that would compete with Weed's *Albany Evening Journal* and present Fillmore's side of the issues.

But at the bottom of Weed's recovery of power was his favored status within the Taylor administration, a problem Fillmore knew he would have to confront. He decided to speak with Taylor directly, not to pressure the President but rather to explain how he was being mistreated. After hearing Fillmore out, the President assured him that he would be treated more justly in the future. Fillmore left the President feeling satisfied that Weed's position with the administration was not as secure as it appeared, and that from now on more of the patronage jobs would go to Fillmore's supporters.

A CRISIS IN THE MAKING

As they spoke, neither Fillmore nor Taylor could know that in less than 10 months their individual actions would greatly alter the course of history. Soon the nation would be so torn with strife that only radical action in Congress could save the Union.

The national crisis grew from a seemingly uncomplicated cause. Congress had to impose some form of government on the vast region the nation had recently acquired from Mexico. But it could not agree on what form this government was to take.

Whigs and Democrats crossed party lines and formed into three separate camps. One group wanted a solution that favored southern ideals and interests; another favored a solution that fit the goals of the northern antislavery movement. The third group, known as the "Nationals," shared the goals of neither the South nor the North. This group took a position that rose above sectional interests in favor of what it felt was best for the nation as a whole.

The President's Solution

Ignoring the fact that his party's support was splintered, President Taylor proposed his own solution. Echoing the position of his team, he recommended that Congress sidestep the entire issue of slavery in the new territory by granting statehood to California and New Mexico and allowing the new states to decide for themselves whether they wanted to be slave or free states.

On hearing of Taylor's proposal, the northerners were overjoyed—but the southerners responded angrily. Some hotheaded southern leaders even called for secession from the Union. How serious this movement was, no one could say for certain, but the violent southern reaction made the "Nationals" pause and reflect on the wisdom of supporting Taylor's plan. Worried about a possible threat to national unity, this group searched for a solution that would satisfy both North and South.

Clay Steps In

Into the growing crisis stepped Henry Clay. In what was to be his last great legislative effort, the great statesman, now 73 and ill, rose in the Senate and announced " a series of resolutions . . . [that will produce] an amiable arrangement of all questions in controversy between the free and slave states, growing out of the subject of slavery."

By proposing this compromise, Clay hoped to point the way to political peace. Basically, Clay's resolutions called for California to be admitted to the Union as a "free" state. New Mexico would be split into two territories rather than granted statehood, with events regarding slavery there allowed to take their natural course without federal intervention. And the Supreme Court would settle the bitter border dispute between Texas and New Mexico.

To further appease the antislavery people, Clay called for abolition of the slave trade in Washington, D.C. And to tempt southerners to support his resolutions, he proposed a new and more effective fugitive slave law.

The Douglas Plan

Clay had set the wheels for compromise in motion. But without the efforts of Stephen A. Douglas, a Democratic senator from Illinois, compromise would have been impossible. Working with his usual energy and intensity—one admirer called him a "steam engine in britches"—Douglas enlisted support from various factions in drafting his own plan.

The Douglas plan differed from Clay's resolutions by ignoring the issues of fugitive slaves, slave trade in the nation's capital, and the Texas-New Mexico border dispute. Instead, Douglas proposed that, in return for admitting California to the Union as a "free" state, the southwest territory be divided into two territories—New Mexico and Utah—and the inhabitants of these territories allowed to decide the issue of slavery for themselves now. They would then decide the slavery issue again when the territories were granted statehood. Douglas' plan proved more acceptable than Clay's to the southerners and also to many "Nationals."

The Omnibus Bill

From his seat in the Senate chamber, Fillmore watched the drama unfold. Because he had been virtually shut out of the Taylor administration's confidence, he could have little direct influence on the nature of the compromise. Instead, he saw his role as that of observer and umpire, and he presided over the debate in the Senate with grace and fairness. Soon, however, through no effort of his own, the territorial issue and Fillmore's fate began to intertwine.

Throughout the spring and early summer of 1850, support for a compromise gained momentum. But the details were still in dispute. Some supporters proposed that the various measures be combined into a so-called "Omnibus Bill." Under this proposal, northerners and southerners alike would have to accept some things they disliked in order to get what they wanted.

As Vice-President, Fillmore presided skillfully over the U.S. Senate during heated debates about the Omnibus Bill, later known as the Compromise of 1850. In this lithograph, published in 1860, Fillmore is shown in the center to the rear, sitting in a large chair, as Senator Daniel Webster (standing at the right) addresses his colleagues. (Library of Congress.)

Problems with Texas

By June, backers of the Omnibus Bill sensed that victory might soon be theirs. But a sudden crisis threatened the bill's successful passage. Texas, correctly fearing that the proposals would remove the New Mexico territory from its domain, moved to secure the territory for itself. But federal troops under the command of a Colonel Monroe met and turned back the Texans. Monroe, acting on direct order from the

President—who strongly opposed the Omnibus Bill and the concessions it made to the southerners—denied the Texas claim and proceeded with steps to make the New Mexico territory a state.

Faced with the prospect of losing 100,000 square miles of land, Texans were enraged. Texas Governor Bell vowed to use force if necessary to regain the territory, and the possibility of a clash between Texas and federal troops became quite real.

The southern states instantly leaped to the side of Texas, and the compromisers rapidly lost ground as extremists on both sides gave new vent to their passions. The chances of passing the Omnibus Bill, which a few weeks before had seemed so good, suddenly withered.

The Deciding Vote

In spite of their fading hopes, Clay and other compromisers moved to push the Omnibus Bill to a vote. As the senators made their positions known, it became more and more possible that Fillmore, in his position as Vice-President and presider over the Senate, would be called upon to break a tie.

When he informed President Taylor of the situation, Fillmore explained that he might have to cast the deciding vote on the Omnibus Bill. As Fillmore recorded later, "If I should feel it my duty to vote for it, as I might, I wished him to understand that it was not out of any hostility to him or his Administration, but that the vote would be given because I deemed it for the interests of the country."

By the time Congress recessed for the Independence Day holiday, the situation had become critical. For seven months Congress had struggled to resolve the national slavery issue.

But just as they were nearing their goal, extremists, led by the President himself, drove a wedge between the two sides—a wedge that possibly could lead to civil war. Although no one knew it at the time, within a week Fillmore would end the crisis.

A FATEFUL MESSAGE

Late Tuesday evening, July 9, 1850, an impatient knock interrupted Fillmore as he disinterestedly read his correspondence. He opened his door to find a breathless messenger from the White House with the expected news: Only minutes before, President Taylor had passed away.

Throughout the evening, Fillmore had been awaiting the message. He had spent most of the afternoon in the dying President's sickroom, and had expected the worst.

Chapter 7

Restoring National Harmony

President Taylor's illness had developed suddenly. On the previous Thursday—Independence Day—he had attended a celebration at the Washington Monument. He sat through several long speeches in the hot sun, then later ate a large bowl of fresh fruit, mostly cherries. By the next morning, he was ill with what his doctor termed "cholera morbus," an intestinal disease. At first no one thought his condition was too serious, but over the weekend he grew weaker, and by Monday he was gravely ill.

THE PRESIDENT "IS NO MORE"

Fillmore first became aware that Taylor was dying late Tuesday morning. In the Senate chamber, while one senator was loudly declaiming the President's stance on the Omnibus Bill, a messenger called Fillmore from his chair. Told that the President was slipping fast, Fillmore hurried out of the chamber to the White House. The messenger then moved about the Senate, whispering the news to Clay, Webster, and several other senators. When they realized the situation, the Senate immediately adjourned.

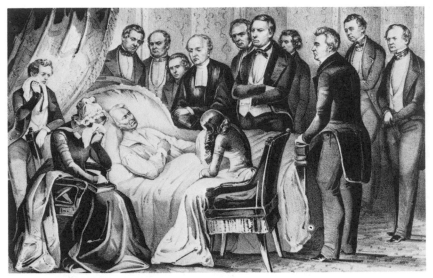

President Taylor died on July 9, 1850, just several days after being stricken with a serious intestinal ailment. On the final day, Vice-President Fillmore and Taylor's family and Cabinet members kept a grim vigil at the dying President's bedside. Fillmore is standing in the center of the group with his arms folded. (Library of Congress.)

At the White House, Fillmore found Taylor's Cabinet officers and other dignitaries assembled in the anteroom outside the President's bedroom. They had all settled down to wait for the outcome. As the afternoon passed, the doctors periodically reported that the President was failing to respond. At the dinner hour, Fillmore went home to get some relief from the tense, oppressive atmosphere in the anteroom. Mrs. Fillmore and Mary had left Washington for Buffalo earlier in the month to escape the capital's summer heat, and so he was alone in the apartment.

Now, as he stood in the doorway of his room at the Willard House, Fillmore read the message from Taylor's Cabinet: "Sir: The . . . painful duty devolves on us to announce to you that Zachary Taylor . . . is no more."

FILLMORE'S RESOLVE

In a moment Fillmore's strength dissolved, and he felt terribly unprepared for the awesome responsibilities that suddenly faced him. He sat down and tried to compose his thoughts, finally sending a message back to the Cabinet: "I have no language to express the emotions of my heart. The shock is so sudden and unexpected that I am overwhelmed. . . . I . . . shall appoint a time and place for taking the oath of office . . . at the earliest moment."

After sending the messenger back to the White House, Fillmore locked his door to all visitors and spent a sleepless night alone. Most Presidents have months before taking office to formulate their policies; Fillmore had but one night. Because the situation between North and South was so tense, his initial actions would be critical. Perhaps no other President ever took office under such difficult circumstances.

As Fillmore reported later, he "reviewed during those hours . . . my own opinions and life." Always, he had had a "feeling, even a prejudice, against slavery." But, after carefully reviewing the political situation, he decided that there was no quick or easy solution to the slavery problem. Instead, to prevent the issue from tearing apart the Union, he resolved to remove it from national politics.

Offering Himself Up

How to accomplish this, Fillmore did not know. But he pledged "to look upon this whole country, from the farthest coast of Maine to the utmost limit of Texas, as but one country" instead of a diverse group of regions with conflicting interests. He would govern accordingly, without favoring one region over another.

Fillmore realized that this policy could damage his own political future. "I well knew that by so doing, I must lose the friendship of many men . . . especially in my own state, and encounter their reproaches." But "to me, this is nothing. The man who can look upon a crisis without being willing to offer himself up upon the altar of this country is not fit for public trust."

THE NEW PRESIDENT

The next morning, July 10, Fillmore officially informed Congress of President Taylor's death. At noon, before a joint session of Congress, Judge William Cranch, chief justice of the U.S. Circuit Court of the District of Columbia, administered the presidential oath of office.

As Fillmore repeated the words of the oath, the congressmen's faces registered mixed emotions. Many tried to hide their uncertainty and fears about the future under a mask of grief, while others struggled to conceal their excitement at what they felt was a coming revolution.

Appointing a Cabinet

On the evening of Fillmore's inauguration, all of Taylor's Cabinet members offered their resignations. Over the past 16 months, they had been at odds with *Vice-President* Fillmore, and now they expected to be dismissed by *President* Fillmore. As he readily accepted their resignations, Fillmore requested that the Cabinet officials stay in office for a month while he found replacements. But they agreed to stay only a week, forcing the new President to work feverishly to assemble a new Cabinet of acceptable advisors.

Under this pressure, Fillmore made some excellent appointments. First, he convinced Daniel Webster to give up his Senate seat to serve as secretary of state. Then, with Web-

*Shortly after assuming the presidency, Fillmore appointed
Daniel Webster as secretary of state. Throughout Fillmore's
term, Webster proved to be an effective and loyal Cabinet
member and advisor.* (Library of Congress.)

ster's help, he quickly filled the other posts. When consider-
ing candidates, Fillmore tested each with the same question:
Was he a Whig with a national rather than a sectional outlook, a man who could see the need for compromise on the
slavery issue?

Omnibus Bill Strategy

After about a week of official mourning, President Fillmore
and Congress turned their attention to the Omnibus Bill. Congress soon learned that the new President had a different attitude toward the bill than his predecessor. Unlike President
Taylor, who had allowed his rigid antislavery stance to move
the nation dangerously close to civil war, President Fillmore
was determined to find a compromise solution that would
avoid war at all costs.

The Omnibus Bill had been devised to discourage Taylor from vetoing (rejecting) measures that he disagreed with
and to encourage sectionalists to vote for certain measures
that were unpopular in their regions in order to get other,
popular measures. Now, with Fillmore in office, the Omnibus Bill was no longer the only possible way to a compromise.

President Fillmore had other ideas. If the bill was broken into several parts, he reasoned, each part could pass or
fail on its own accord, and the administration would not have
to force acceptance of particular measures or the entire pack-
age. In other words, by staying out of the congressional debate on the Omnibus Bill and letting the sectionalists and the
"Nationals" decide the separate issues themselves, the administration could act as a peacemaker in Congress and in the nation at large.

Following this strategy, Daniel Webster called for enactment of the entire Omnibus Bill or, if that failed, then the
immediate acceptance of its measures in separate bills. At

the same time, Fillmore announced that he would sign any constitutionally sound measure passed by Congress. He then waited for Congress, now freed of the threat of a presidential veto, to take one or the other road toward peace.

The Dawson Proviso

Within a week of Fillmore's announcement, the Senate was ready to vote on the Omnibus Bill. But Henry Clay, in an attempt to win a few more votes, made one last modification in the bill. This change, known as the Dawson Proviso, proposed to postpone a settlement of the Texas boundary dispute with New Mexico and then to determine it not by legislative enactment, but by the findings of a special committee.

Through the Dawson Proviso, Clay hoped to give southern sectionalists the impression that much of the New Mexico territory would one day be part of Texas, and therefore additional slave territory. At first, his strategy seemed to work, as the Senate readily accepted the Dawson Proviso.

But Clay actually had made a mistake. In altering the Omnibus Bill, he had misinterpreted Fillmore's true goal. Since the Dawson Proviso failed to settle the Texas boundary dispute, it left open the way for Texas to assert its claim to the New Mexico territory with armed force.

The Compromise of 1850

Seeing the dangers of the revised Omnibus Bill, Fillmore moved quickly to restore its original decisive language on the Texas boundary issue. He and his advisors laid out a simple strategy: either eliminate the Dawson Proviso from the Omnibus Bill or else clear the way for a complete settlement by breaking up the bill into separate parts.

After a prolonged, heated Senate debate, Fillmore achieved his goal. Measure after measure was struck from the Omnibus Bill, until all that was left was a simple reorganization of Utah. In the final analysis, the Omnibus Bill had been broken up because of Fillmore's desire for peace.

Almost immediately, the pieces of Fillmore's grand plan began to fall into place. A revised Texas boundary bill, which gave Texas 33,000 square miles of the New Mexico territory, was passed after Fillmore's personal appeal to Congress. In rapid succession, Congress then enacted four more measures: admitted California to the Union as a free state on September 9; established the territories of New Mexico and Utah, also on September 9; passed the Fugitive Slave Act, an amendment of the Slave Act of 1793; and abolished the slave trade in Washington, D.C. Collectively, these five measures became known as the Compromise of 1850.

Except for the Fugitive Slave Act, Fillmore signed each bill almost as soon as it reached his desk. On this act, however, he hesitated. But although he found its measures — involving the rights of slaveholders to recapture runaway slaves — repugnant, he felt duty-bound to uphold the Constitution at all costs, and so eventually he signed it.

When the dust had settled and the compromise measures had all passed, the clouds of conflict and disunion that had been hovering over the nation disappeared. In 10 short weeks, Fillmore had apparently solved the territorial disputes that had plagued the nation for the past four years.

A Comforting Family

Almost as soon as they heard the news of President Taylor's death, Fillmore's wife and children had set out on the long journey from Buffalo to Washington. Although they arrived too late for the hastily arranged inauguration ceremony, their presence helped the new President become adjusted to the demands of the office.

Nicknamed Abby, Fillmore's daughter Mary Abigail helped her ailing mother with the social duties expected of a First Lady.
(Library of Congress.)

Unfortunately, Abigail Fillmore was ill and not able to perform all the customary social duties of a First Lady. But their lovely and talented daughter Mary, just 19, pitched in to help. Young Millard, already a lawyer, became his father's private secretary.

NEW TROUBLE IN NEW YORK

Fillmore's family was his only comfort, however. He had hoped that the Compromise of 1850 would bring automatic peace in Congress, but these hopes were proving unfounded.

It was becoming apparent that if true peace was to prevail, he would have to persuade even the most radical sectionalists to accept the measures. In the meantime, his old adversaries, Thurlow Weed and William Seward, were poised to foil his efforts.

No Revenge

For more than a year, Weed and Seward had engaged in open political warfare with Vice-President Fillmore. Throughout that period, Fillmore had fought back effectively, rallying Whigs throughout New York state behind him. But Weed had remained confident that his and Seward's growing influence with the Taylor administration would destroy whatever influence Fillmore still retained.

When the news of Taylor's death reached New York, Weed was devastated. In one stroke, the man he had sought to destroy now commanded the entire federal government. Weed was sure that Fillmore would use his new position to take revenge by dismissing the political appointees he had used his influence to obtain.

But once again, Weed and Seward misjudged Fillmore. Vengefulness simply was not part of the new President's character. Feeling politically secure and mindful of the more important national concerns facing his administration, Fillmore had no desire to carry out a personal vendetta against his old rivals. Rather, he felt that his political life had reached its apex and that he had a great obligation to the nation. He was committed, with an honesty that none could doubt, to a policy of restoring national harmony. Fullfilling that committment would leave little time or energy for involvement in New York politics.

Weed Tries Again

In the first three months of his administration, Fillmore withdrew only one Weed political appointment. He hoped that this restraint would help convince Weed and Seward to abandon their attempts at arousing sectional unrest in the North and bring them into line behind his policies. However, time would soon show that his attitude towards the two was based on misplaced hopes. Despite their outward show of conciliation with Fillmore, Weed and Seward actually harbored dreams of using their control of the New York Whig Party as a springboard to greater national political influence. They soon devised a strategy to achieve this goal.

Less than a week after the final Compromise of 1850 measure was passed, New York Whigs held a state nominating convention at Syracuse. As the convention progressed, Weed's strategy became clear: disrupt the convention and split the party. At first, he had some success. A group of Fillmore supporters — known as the "Silver Grays" because of the flowing gray hair of their leader, Francis Granger — stalked out of the convention hall in dispute over Weed-initiated resolutions that clashed with the measures in the Compromise of 1850.

But shortly afterwards, a group of wealthy New York City merchants, both Whigs and Democrats, favoring the compromise measures and strongly opposing Weed and his actions, created the "Union Association" to — in the words of its manifesto — "take any action best calculated to avert the further progress of political agitation in the north." The Union Association quickly gained influence in the state, attracting many wealthy and powerful citizens with its philosophy of moderation, restraint, and preservation of the union.

This development pleased Fillmore greatly — as did the

results of the state election in November 1850, which dealt a serious blow to Weed and Seward's hopes. In business circles, the results brought celebration because reports revealed that southerners had interpreted New York's election as a decisive blow against Seward and agitation, and as a victory for the Union and the compromise. In one stroke, Fillmore had achieved two important goals: thwarting Weed and gaining his home state's endorsement of the compromise. He had not only outmaneuvered Weed in a political game at which Weed was a master, he had also succeeded in expanding support for his policies.

THE FUGITIVE SLAVE ACT

Fillmore's battle for sectional peace and national unity required his constant attention. Abolition and antislavery advocates had been steadily gaining popular support over the past several years. Now they turned their attention to the Fugitive Slave Act and then to President Fillmore himself.

Because it required constant enforcement, the Fugitive Slave Act gave antislavery leaders plenty of opportunity to challenge it in practice. The leaders attacked the act and denounced Fillmore for signing it. The President even received some anonymous death threats from angry fanatics.

An Appeasement to Southerners

Basically, the Fugitive Slave Act was merely a modification of an existing law, created in 1793, that authorized a slaveowner to pursue and seize a runaway slave in any state in the Union and, after satisfying identification requirements, to bring the

The Fugitive Slave Act

One of the most controversial measures of the Compromise of 1850 was the Fugitive Slave Act. Among its provisions, the act appointed paid federal commissioners to help ensure the return of runaway slaves to their owners. Under the direction of these commissioners, U.S. marshals could arrest and jail fugitives pending decision on whether the slaveholder's claim was valid. The marshals could also call out posses to help track down runaway slaves and to protect against mobs trying to free jailed fugitives. They even protected slaveowners transporting their runaways back to the South.

Perhaps more than any other issue, the Fugitive Slave Act aroused antislavery sentiment throughout the North. Despite the efforts of conservative northerners to stem the abolitionist fever sweeping the region, radical opposition to the act grew and was soon translated into action.

The states of Massachusetts and Wisconsin took the lead in opposing the act. Massachusetts, in particular, produced a great number of radical "Free Soilers"—people opposed to extending slavery into any new U.S. territories and dedicated to abolishing slavery in existing states. Men such as Horace Mann, Senator Charles Sumner, and Dr. Samuel Gridley Howe, although basically conservatives in most issues, became increasingly willing to work with radical abolitionists such as Lysander Spooner, whose *A Defence for Fugi-*

tive Slaves outlined methods of circumventing the Fugitive Slave Act and helping escaped slaves remain free.

In 1850 Boston became the scene of a famous challenge to the Fugitive Slave Act. Two years earlier, the Underground Railroad (a network of routes over which slaves could escape to Canada) had brought slaves William and Ellen Crofts to Boston. Since no fugitive had been returned to the South from Massachusetts for many years, it was thought to be a safe haven. Abolitionist newspapers gleefully announced the Crofts' escape and dared the slaveowner, Robert Collins of Macon, Georgia, to do anything about it. At first, Collins dared not act. But in 1850, after passage of the Fugitive Slave Act, he decided to send two slave-catchers to Boston to bring the Crofts back to Georgia.

When news of the slave-catchers' intentions reached Boston, the abolitionists decided that, rather than send the Crofts out of the country to safety, they would publicly challenge the act. They hid the Crofts in the homes of two elite Boston families and held a large public meeting to protest the act. A committee for the Crofts' defense, which included some of Boston's highest ranking officials, repeatedly obstructed the slave-catchers' efforts, having them arrested three times on trumped-up charges.

Into the middle of this chaos stepped President Fillmore, who announced his intention to enforce the Fugitive Slave Act at all costs — with federal troops, if necessary. Rather than risk the intervention of troops and jeopardize the Crofts' freedom, the abolitionists hid the couple on a ship bound for London. The Crofts sailed away safely, and the slave-catchers returned to Georgia empty-handed.

Fillmore's actions did not return the slaves to their owner, but they did demonstrate his resolve to enforce the law and uphold the spirit of compromise. To abolitionists, however, his name became shrouded with infamy.

slave back home. The Fugitive Slave Act of 1850 expanded on the 1793 law to give federal law enforcement agencies increased responsibility and manpower to pursue, capture, and return escaped slaves. For political reasons, Fillmore had agreed to include it in the Compromise of 1850 — mainly to appease the southerners.

The antislavery movement's first challenge to the Fugitive Slave Act came not long after the new law was enacted. In Pennsylvania, an antislavery mob defied a federal marshal's authority by storming a jail in which the marshal held a runaway slave, overpowering the guards, and whisking the slave away to freedom. Faced with this challenge to the law and his authority, Fillmore reluctantly decided to use federal troops to help enforce the law in future instances.

A Distaste for Slavery

Despite his endorsement of the Fugitive Slave Act and his determination to enforce it, Fillmore had a basic distaste for slavery. But once again, his primary goal of preserving the

Union overcame his personal antislavery sentiments. His attitude is revealed in a letter he wrote to Daniel Webster:

> God knows that I detest slavery, but it is an existing evil, for which we are not responsible, and we must endure it, and give it such protection as is guaranteed by the Constitution, till we can get rid of it without destroying the last hope of government in the free world. My object, however, has been to avoid the use of military force as far as possible, not doubting that there is yet patriotism enough left in every State north of Mason's and Dixon's line to maintain the supremacy of the laws; and being particularly anxious that no State should be disgraced, by being compelled to resort to the army to support the laws of the Union, if it could be avoided. I have therefore commenced mildly — authorizing this force only in the last resort, but if necessary, I shall not hesitate to give greater power, and finally to bring the whole force of the government to sustain the law.

Although Fillmore hoped that the antislavery agitators would cease without federal intervention, protests and slave rescues increased. In response, he increased federal involvement in runaway slave cases — and even became personally involved in one case. Determination to enforce the law was not Fillmore's only motive for doing so; he also was becoming concerned over a growing radicalism in the South.

DISCONTENT IN THE SOUTH

To many southerners, the Compromise of 1850 represented a complete defeat that had reduced the South to a position of inferiority. Except for the Fugitive Slave Act, every measure went against them and for the North. The South had lost California, would probably lose New Mexico and Utah, had failed to expand Texas as much as it wanted, and had lost on the slave trade in Washington. Many southerners could see, given the developments in the North, that the Fugitive Slave Act would soon be in peril. A growing resentment fueled southern thoughts and talk of secession from the Union.

A Meeting in Nashville

Early advocates of secession—led by the governors of Georgia, Mississippi, and South Carolina—called a convention of southern leaders in Nashville, Tennessee, for early November 1850. Here, they hoped to funnel all the southern discontent into a movement strong enough to challenge President Fillmore's cherished solidarity.

But before the convention in Nashville could take place, a strong effort by southern "National" Whigs—now calling themselves the "Union and Southern Rights Party"—helped candidates who supported the Compromise of 1850 carry the state elections in Georgia. This Union Party victory quickly cooled the radicals' fire, and few paid much attention to the fiery speeches and calls for secession that filled the hall at the convention in Nashville. Back in Washington, President Fillmore and his advisors breathed more easily.

Chapter 8

A New Era of Prosperity

By the summer of 1851, the national mood had changed somewhat. A calm had settled over the land, interrupted only occasionally by an outburst of sentiment for or against slavery. The nation appeared to be tired of sectional disputes, and the spirit of the Compromise of 1850 was becoming accepted as the national destiny.

In the South, where the danger of secession had been real, if brief, much credit was given to President Fillmore for averting the crisis. A period of prosperity, with cotton selling for 13 cents a pound, also helped to defuse the unrest.

DOMESTIC EXPANSION

With relative harmony achieved, Fillmore tried to direct the nation's attention to other matters. As a devout Whig, he championed increased industrial and commercial growth and advocated expanding the nation's transportation networks.

As if taking its inspiration from the President, the nation as a whole entered a new era of prosperity. Industrial development boomed and the cities exploded in size. Railroads replaced canals as the main mode of transporting goods and people, opening the midwestern prairies to settlement. Along with economic expansion came a new style of living, celebrating the luxurious and ornate, worshipping the pursuit of material wealth, and disdaining the "common" and the "vulgar."

The Fillmores slipped easily into the ostentatious living of the day, helped by the wealthy merchants and manufacturers who were grateful for all the President had done to preserve the Union—and, of course, the favorable business climate. For instance, one group of New York City merchants gave the First Lady a magnificent coach and a pair of horses. The coach, custom-crafted and almost embarrassingly ornate, cost over $1,500—a staggering sum in 1851.

FOREIGN AFFAIRS

During his administration, Fillmore's attitude towards foreign nations clearly harmonized with his policies at home. His concern for railroads, canals, rivers, harbors, and uniform, sound currency—the foundations of national commerce—had shaped his political outlook from the start. So, too, had his belief that one of government's primary functions was to encourage and aid business. So it came as no surprise when he began to apply these beliefs and policies to foreign markets.

Fillmore's foreign policy was very simple: promote, by honorable means, every legitimate interest of American business overseas. During his short time in office, he aggressively promoted various business interests. But despite all of his aggressiveness in these ventures, he never yielded to the temptation to use America's power for imperialistic land-grabbing. Seizing overseas colonies just did not fit into his plans for expanding American commerce and maintaining domestic peace.

Building a Highway to the Orient

As President, Fillmore had inherited the responsibility of promoting American trade in the Orient against its main rival, the British. One way he hoped to do so was by encouraging the development of railroad and canal routes across Central America that linked the Caribbean Sea and the Pacific Ocean. Three routes were under consideration: Panama, Nicaragua, and southern Mexico. A private concern was already building a railroad across Panama. President Fillmore reported to Congress in December 1851 that "a considerable part of the railroad has been completed . . . mail and passengers will in the future be conveyed thereon."

When Fillmore took office, American promoters were surveying a railroad route across Mexico's extreme southern region. But although he pledged his administration's aid to the project, and intervened several times with the Mexican government on behalf of the contractors, the project sank beneath the weight of complex business and political rivalries.

A canal project proved to be even more difficult to launch than a railroad. At the time, a canal through Panama was thought to be impractical, and the site was deemed suited only for a railroad. A canal through the southern part of Mexico was totally infeasible because of the great distance involved. Engineers of the day thought that the only possible canal route lay through Nicaragua; but the British presence and a later revolution squelched any hopes for such a canal.

Protecting Hawaii

American expansion into the Pacific Ocean and to the Orient made the Hawaiian Islands a natural point of interest. Bringing the islands under the American sphere of influence and keeping it out of foreign hands became a major goal of the Fillmore administration. As Fillmore later recounted:

We were influenced in this measure by the existing and prospective importance of the islands as a place of refuge and refreshment for our vessels engaged in whale fishing, and by the consideration that they lie in the course of the great trade which must at no distant day be carried on between the western coast of North America and eastern Asia.

By 1851, a movement to annex the Hawaiian Islands to the United States was gaining momentum. The Hawaiian king himself offered Fillmore the opportunity for annexation. The President resisted such pressure, however, preferring to keep the islands independent.

Meanwhile, the French attempted to gain the islands for themselves. They had seized Honolulu in 1848, although they later withdrew, and in 1851 presented the king with a list of demands that would essentially make the islands a French protectorate. The Fillmore administration reacted swiftly and decisively, with Daniel Webster sharply informing Napoleon III that Hawaii must remain independent and, if it were to lose its independence, it would be to the United States. Unwilling to force a confrontation, the French withdrew.

Opening Japan

For more than 200 years, Japan had kept its ports closed to foreign trade, except for one small harbor where the Dutch were permitted to operate a limited business. In the meantime, trade between China and the United States had skyrocketed. Farsighted businessmen began looking to Japan both as a fuel station for steamships on their way to and from China and as a rich new market for American goods and materials.

Once in office, Fillmore encouraged renewed efforts at opening Japan to western trade. In December 1852, he dispatched four warships under Commodore Matthew C. Perry

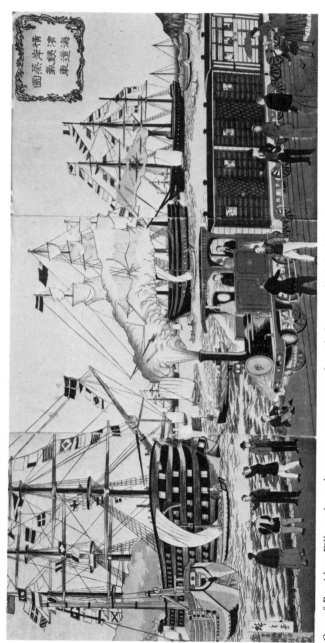

One of President Fillmore's goals was to open up trade with Japan, which had kept its ports almost totally closed to foreign trade for more than 200 years. Toward this end, in December 1852, Fillmore sent four ships to Japan under the command of Commodore Matthew C. Perry. This woodblock print by a Japanese artist shows Perry's ships in the harbor of Yokohama, along with a scaled-down locomotive and passenger cars that Perry brought for the amusement of his hosts. (Library of Congress.)

to Japan with instructions to obtain from the Japanese government pledges to aid shipwrecked American sailors, to provide U.S. vessels with coal and other supplies, and to open at least one port to U.S. trade. Perry eventually won these concessions in the Treaty of Kanagawa, signed in 1854, which opened two Japanese ports for U.S. trade.

Fillmore's administration had prepared the ground for sweeping changes between the East and the West, and his highway to the Orient was taking shape.

Obstructing Manifest Destiny

Despite his firm conviction that American commerce should be given every encouragement to expand around the globe, Fillmore was no believer in Manifest Destiny—the doctrine of aggressive territorial expansion that many Americans regarded as a birthright. To Fillmore, it was honorable to use his presidential authority to promote commerce, but dishonorable to seize another country's land.

Fillmore's policies regarding Manifest Destiny received several challenges during his time in office. The first, improbably enough, revolved around a group of remote islands off the coast of Peru. These islands, barren and uninhabited, contained one commodity that made them extremely valuable. For centuries, sea birds had used the islands as a nesting place, and their excrement—called guano—had built up to depths of 30 feet in some places.

Highly prized as a plant fertilizer, guano brought a handsome price. For decades, ships from the United States and other nations had transported loads of guano from the islands to markets all over the world. Until 1850, the Peruvian government did little to enforce its ownership of the islands. But then, a revolution brought into power a new regime that threatened to fire on any ship coming to the islands in search of guano.

Calling in the Navy

Meanwhile, a group of influential New York businessmen had proposed sending a hundred ships to the Peruvian islands to haul away thousands of tons of guano. Concerned that the Peruvian government would try to stop them, the group asked Daniel Webster to arrange for protection by the U.S. Navy. Webster readily complied.

Hearing of the enterprise, the Peruvian minister to the United States complained, and the affair came to Fillmore's attention. Not knowing of Webster's promise of naval protection, Fillmore reviewed the matter. He decided that the islands were rightfully Peru's and that the United States could not protect Americans if they tried to take guano without the Peruvian government's consent. But his decision came after the fleet had already set sail. Fearing that without federal protection their enterprise could be doomed, the New York group exerted extreme political pressure on Fillmore.

Although the President finally gave into the group's pressure, he had set a precedent that would prevent this group and other speculators from freely exploiting foreign assets in the future. Fillmore also could gain satisfaction from his defense of the nation's honor, which he strove to keep untarnished.

Fillmore successfully obstructed Manifest Destiny in other regions as well. On April 25, 1851, he issued a proclamation warning foreign countries against participation in expeditions against Cuba. In October of that same year, he issued a similar proclamation regarding forays into Mexico.

ANOTHER TERM?

On December 7, 1851, Fillmore's old Buffalo friend, Dr. Thomas Foote, paused before the White House door. He had traveled as rapidly as possible to Washington in response to a letter he carried in his pocket—a letter from the President summoning him to the White House. Upon entering Fillmore's study, Dr. Foote found his old friend reading some state papers, awaiting his arrival. After a warm greeting, Fillmore stated the reason for summoning Foote: he had decided to withdraw from the presidential race of 1852.

A Personal Decision

In truth, Fillmore had made this decision some 17 months earlier, shortly after he had succeeded Zachary Taylor as President. He had no desire to succeed himself. As he later recalled:

> When I was called to the Presidency, the country was agitated by political and sectional passions . . .patriots and statesmen looked with apprehension about the future. . . . I was oppressed by a sense of the great responsibilities that rested upon me, and sincerely distrusted my ability. To prepare and strengthen myself . . . I endeavored to lay aside . . . every personal ambition.

Not wishing to weaken the Whig Party or the Compromise of 1850 effort, Fillmore had kept his decision to himself. But although he sincerely did not want to run, political circumstances drew him into the race. In the South, Whigs aligned with the Union Party could see no other worthy candidate. And the move to nominate Fillmore was not limited to the South. From the North and West also came endorsements and pledges of support. The move to nominate Fillmore gained so much strength that Thurlow Weed threw up his hands in desperation. Convinced that he could not stem the tide for Fillmore, Weed set sail for Europe, content to sit out the 1852 presidential election campaign.

Bright Prospects

Eventually, driven by a gnawing sense of responsibility to the party and the nation, Fillmore consented to allow his name to be placed in nomination at the Whig National Convention in Baltimore. His prospects looked bright and became even brighter when none other than Henry Clay, the old Whig warhorse, gave his endorsement to Fillmore. Seriously ill – in fact, dying – Clay roused himself to make a deathbed appeal for his party to nominate Fillmore.

But Fillmore's political enemies were busy at work as well. William Seward and his allies endorsed General Winfield Scott for the nomination, not out of a desire to see him win it, but out of a desire to defeat Fillmore. With Fillmore out of the way, the Sewardites would be in control of the convention and could even nominate Seward himself.

Fillmore's Dilemma

As the convention neared, Fillmore found himself faced with a dilemma. If he stayed in the race and won the nomination, by all accounts he would probably lose the election. But if he withdrew from the race before the nomination, the convention would fall into the hands of the Sewardites, who could use it as a means to drive the moderate "Nationals" from the Whig Party and set the stage for a successful Seward campaign in 1856.

Fillmore's choice was simple – the loss of personal dignity or party discord. Since he was thoroughly convinced of the rightness of the Compromise of 1850 and of the need for party harmony, Fillmore swallowed his pride and set out for Baltimore.

Convention Defeat

The convention opened on Wednesday, June 16, in steamy midsummer Baltimore. Over the next two days the convention hall and nearby hotels and taverns buzzed with political skirmishes and back-room dealings. Finally, the convention decided on a party platform (stand on issues) that endorsed the Compromise of 1850 measures – a victory for the Fillmorites.

At this point, feeling satisfied that the party was on the right track, Fillmore wanted to withdraw. He asked that his delegates be transferred to Daniel Webster if possible. But Fillmore's friends, sensing victory, declined to accept his withdrawal.

Balloting to determine the nominee began late Friday evening. By Monday morning, the convention was deadlocked and the nomination was still up in the air. Complicating matters was Webster's candidacy.

Even though Webster could attract only 29 votes (compared to Fillmore's 133 and Scott's 131), the stubborn old campaigner refused to withdraw from the race. He felt humiliated that after 42 years of public service, he could get only such a meager number of votes. Webster hung on in the hope that Fillmore would indeed withdraw and he would inherit his delegates. Finally, after party delegations convinced Webster that his refusal to withdraw was only taking votes away from Fillmore, he had a change of heart.

But Webster's decision came too late. Monday morning, on the convention's 48th ballot, two Fillmore delegates switched to Scott. It was now time for Webster's votes to be transferred to Fillmore. But the Webster delegates were in disarray, and many went over to Scott. On the 53rd ballot, Scott received more than the 147 votes required and was nominated.

DEATH OF A PARTY

Scott's victory left Fillmore unruffled — after all, he had not sought the nomination anyway. But the Whig Party was in an uproar. Two days after the nomination, a conference of southern Whigs held in Washington resolved not to vote for Scott under any circumstances. In all quarters, the nomination was seen as a death blow to the party. "National" Whigs in particular considered the party now broken beyond repair.

The national election in November 1852 confirmed their fears. Scott carried only four states, while the Democrat candidate, Franklin Pierce, won the other 27. For all practical purposes, the Whig Party was no more.

Chapter 9

Later Years

After failing in his bid for the Whig presidential nomination, Fillmore spent the fall and winter of 1852 in relative calm. Seldom had a President passed his final days in office in such a serene and unruffled manner, without a crisis or a significant incident. Even the slavery question seemed almost forgotten.

The atmosphere of calm was broken only once, by the death of Daniel Webster in October. After mourning his old compatriot, Fillmore turned his attention to his life after the White House.

RETIREMENT CONCERNS

Concerned that a former President should live in a manner that upheld the dignity of the office—and feeling that his modest frame house in Buffalo would not do—Fillmore instructed his old friend and partner, Nathan Hall, to "look around Buffalo for a suitable house."

Fillmore also was concerned about a source of income. Unlike most other retiring Presidents, he had no gentleman's estate or family business to fall back on. He had enough savings and investments on which to live comfortably, but not to support him and his family in a manner befitting their position. After several months of deliberation, he decided to return to the law profession, confining his practice to the highest courts and most important cases in order to maintain his dignity.

Meanwhile, Fillmore's friends and supporters strove to convince him not to retire from politics. At first he resisted, but as he pondered his position and the direction the nation seemed to be taking, he confided to Nathan Hall that he indeed had a "political future" in mind. The nature of that future, however, was anything but clear.

ABIGAIL DIES

March 4, 1853 – Inauguration Day – brought wet snow and gusty winds to the nation's capital. The swearing-in ceremony which Fillmore and Abigail attended, as was customary, was held outside on the steps of the Capitol. As he watched new President Franklin Pierce take the oath of office, Fillmore glanced over at his wife to see how she was faring.

Although Abigail was braving the weather with a determined, if weak, smile, her lips were blue and her face pale and drawn. She had been ailing for several months, and exposure to this raw weather could only do her harm.

Following the ceremony, Fillmore escorted President Pierce back to the White House and then hurriedly returned to the Willard House, where the Fillmores had taken some rooms for several days after the inauguration. To his relief, Abigail appeared tired but otherwise well. But by the next morning, it became obvious that she had caught a bad cold. By night, she was running a high fever, and the cold quickly developed into pneumonia. Hour after hour, Fillmore and his son and daughter sat at her bedside, hoping for signs of improvement. But slowly she slipped away. On March 30, after three weeks of illness, Abigail Fillmore died.

The next day, the grief-stricken family set out with Abigail's body for Buffalo, where she was buried the following day. For Fillmore, all plans for a gracious life, a "political future," and eventual comfortable retirement dissolved in grief and depression.

A NEW POLITICAL PARTY

For the first few months after Abigail's death, Fillmore retreated into the family home on Franklin Street and contemplated his past and future. Reading, writing, and surveying the political scene occupied his lonely days. Soon, he began looking for a way back into the political arena.

He did not have to look very far. Over the past several years, a new phenomenon had come onto the American political scene. Starting with the creation of "nativist" clubs in New York City, such as the Order of the Star-Spangled Banner, a movement aimed at oppressing "foreigners" (actually meaning recent immigrants) and Catholics was sweeping the nation.

The Know-Nothings

By 1854 the Order of the Star-Spangled Banner had grown into a full-fledged political party. Although its leaders took the name "American Party," the public referred to it as the "Know-Nothing Party" because in its previously secret political activities its members had protected themselves and their group by claiming, when questioned, "I know nothing about it."

Gradually, as their own party broke apart, many old "National" Whigs gravitated to the Know-Nothings. Fillmore himself, driven as always by his all-consuming desire to preserve

The Know-Nothings:
The One-Issue Party

Fear and hostility toward immigrants is nothing new in the United States. Established Americans have always had uncertain feelings about those who came later. Even George Washington tempered his belief that "the bosom of American is always open to receive not only the opulent and respectable stranger, but the oppressed and persecuted of all nations" by limiting his welcome to those "who by decency and propriety of conduct . . . seem to merit [it]."

These traditional "nativist" sentiments might have been manageable had most of the immigrants been Prostestant, for until the mid-1800s, American remained an overwhelmingly Protestant nation. But the tide of Irish-Catholic immigrants—216,000 in 1851 alone—frightened even moderate Protestants. Tales of the newcomers' illiteracy, laziness, and love of alcohol and political agitation sparked the formation of secret anti-Catholic societies such as the "Order of the Star-Spangled Banner" in New York City. Soon, rhetoric turned into violence. Nativist mobs attacked Irish tenements and even Catholic churches and convents, and many lives were lost.

In 1854 several antiimmigrant groups merged to form the American Party, better known as the Know-Nothings because members were pledged to reply "I know nothing" when questioned about the party's secret activities. Vowing to bar Catholics and immigrants from holding public office and proposing other antiimmigrant policies, the party became wildly—if briefly—popular. Stores sold "Know-Nothing Candy," "Know-Nothing Tea," and "Know-Nothing Toothpicks," among other items, and a clipper ship launched in New York in 1854 was christened the *Know-Nothing*.

By 1855, Know-Nothing candidates held 48 seats in the U.S. Congress, and the party nominated former President Fillmore as their candidate for the 1856 presidential election. However, Fillmore carried only one state— Maryland—and like most one-issue parties, the Know-Nothings disintegrated shortly thereafter.

the Union, eyed the Know-Nothings as a possible vehicle for reviving the "National" Whig program. But until the new party proved that it could win elections, he withheld his support.

The fall elections of 1854 showed just how powerful the Know-Nothings were becoming. Throughout the previous summer, its membership had grown phenomenally, and its leaders looked forward to the upcoming election with confidence. The election results justified their confidence. Know-Nothing candidates won seats in almost every state: only in the West was the new party weak.

Another Death in the Family

Just when Fillmore decided to make himself available as a presidential candidate of the Know-Nothing Party is unclear. But the sudden and unexpected death of his daughter Mary at the end of July 1854 may have influenced his decision. Mary had been in perfect health, and on the very evening before her death had been in her usual high spirits. But within a few hours of the first signs of illness she died, at the age of only 22.

Fillmore's grief was profound. Possibly to lift him out of it, he turned back to politics. Although he did not share much of the philosophy or overall aims of the Know-Nothings — he was much more concerned with promoting national unity than with blaming foreigners and Catholics for the nation's problems — he understood that a strong spirit of nativism could perhaps serve as a rallying point around which a reborn "National" Whig Party could gather.

The Election of 1856

On New Year's Day 1855, Fillmore announced his intention to seek the Know-Nothing nomination for the 1856 presidential election. The decision made, he then embarked on a 12-month tour of Europe. While he idled away his time talking with kings, tasting continental cuisine, and seeing the sights, his friends back in the United States worked hard on behalf of his candidacy. They arranged for a gala ceremony on Fillmore's return from overseas to mark the beginning of his campaign.

In his first speech of the campaign, Fillmore outlined his position and promised . . .

> . . . a faithful and impartial administration of the laws of the country. If there be those either North or South who desire an administration for the North as against the South, or for the South as against the North, they are not the men who should give their suffrages to me. For my own part, I know only my country, my whole country, and nothing but my country.

Although he really did not share the party's philosophy or overall aims, being more interested in resurrecting the national Whig Party, Fillmore accepted the American, or "Know-Nothing," Party's nomination as its presidential candidate for the election of 1856. He was soundly defeated, however, garnering just 21 percent of the total vote. (Library of Congress.)

Despite his campaigning, Fillmore's chances for victory dimmed as the summer went on. Although he also gained the endorsement of the remnants of the Whig Party, in the November election Fillmore drew just 21 percent of the vote, running third behind John C. Fremont and the winner, James Buchanan.

BUFFALO'S FIRST CITIZEN

The 1856 election returns, although disappointing, came as no shock to Fillmore. Looking at the results and searching within himself, he declared that his political career was finally at an end. But what was the future to hold, if not politics?

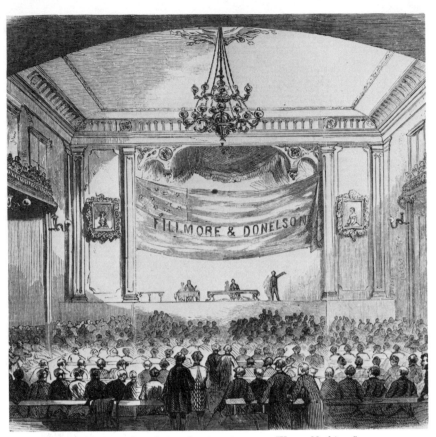

This wood engraving shows the American, or "Know-Nothing," Party's 1856 national convention in Louisville, Kentucky, at which Fillmore accepted the party's presidential nomination. (Library of Congress.)

A Second Marriage

One answer came in the form of romance. On February 10, 1858, Fillmore married the former Mrs. Caroline Carmichael MacIntosh, the 52-year-old widow of a wealthy merchant. Gracious and cultured, Caroline soon gained acceptance among Fillmore's wide circle of friends and Buffalo society. The newlyweds purchased a stately mansion on Niagara Square, which soon became a center of Buffalo's society life.

Caroline Carmichael MacIntosh, the widow of a wealthy Buf-falo merchant, became Fillmore's second wife on February 10, 1858. (Library of Congress.)

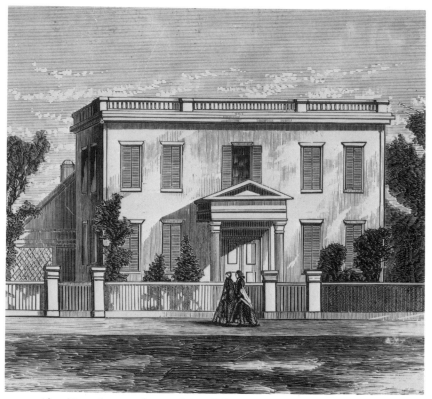

After his retirement from politics, Fillmore turned his attention to serving the Buffalo community. He and Caroline moved into a stately mansion on Niagara Square, which became a center of Buffalo's social scene. (Library of Congress.)

CIVIL WAR

Another answer came with the onset of the Civil War. With southern secession and the war, Fillmore's greatest fears had been realized. Throughout his long political career, he had opposed any act that might lead to disunion. Now, he un-hesitatingly gave of his time, his money, and his heart to the cause of a war to re-establish the Union.

One day after President Lincoln had called for volunteers for the Union Army, Fillmore led a gigantic demonstration, at which he declared:

> My fellow citizens, it is no time for any man to shrink from the responsibility which events have cast upon him. We have reached a crisis . . . when no man has a right to stand neutral. Civil War has been inaugurated, and we must meet it. Our Constitution is in danger, and we must defend it.

The rally was only a beginning. Fillmore soon organized the "Union Continentals," a company in the New York militia made up of retired militia officers. The members all dressed in colorful uniforms and trained in ceremonial routines. Whenever an affair needed a show of patriotism or pomp, the Union Continentals were there to provide it. They led Buffalo war volunteers down to the railroad station, marched in funerals, and led Fourth of July parades.

After the war ended, Fillmore turned his attention and considerable energies to serving the Buffalo community. He became the city's patriarch, a role he thoroughly enjoyed. Unselfishly, he gave his talents to numerous causes—economic growth, education, health care, the arts, historic preservation, and even animal welfare (as a vice-president of the local Society for the Prevention of Cruelty to Animals).

FILLMORE PASSES ON

Although each year Fillmore's hair grew whiter and his step less bouncy, he remained in remarkably good health as he entered his seventies. As late as January 1874, he could brag to a friend, "My health is perfect, I eat, drink, and sleep as well as ever, and take a deep but silent interest in public affairs."

But on the morning of February 13, as he was shaving, Fillmore suffered a stroke that paralyzed his left hand. The paralysis soon affected the left side of his face. Two weeks later he suffered another attack, which destroyed any hope he had of recovery. Then, on March 8, he died peacefully in his sleep.

Two days later, Fillmore's body was removed from the mansion on Niagara Square. Hundreds of mourners, including his wife and son, followed the funeral procession down Delaware Avenue to Forest Lawn Cemetery, where he was buried.

A later Buffalo generation, better able to evaluate Fillmore's work on behalf of the nation and his community, erected a statue of their first citizen in front of City Hall. Today, this statue still looks upon the city that Millard Fillmore helped to forge and that helped shape his destiny. But its cold stone obscures the warmth and wisdom that the 13th President of the United States brought to his defense of the Union.

Bibliography

Nevins, Allan. *Ordeal of the Union: Fruits of Manifest Destiny.* New York: Scribner's, 1947. This book provides background information on mid-19th century America and discusses Fillmore's role in shaping the policies of the time.

Rayback, Robert J. *Millard Fillmore: Biography of a President.* Buffalo, NY: Henry Stewart, 1959. This long and detailed book is the best biography of Millard Fillmore available.

Seale, William. *The President's House: A History.* Washington, D.C.: White House Historical Association, 1986. This beautiful two-volume set focuses mainly on the White House itself, but it also contains many interesting details about Fillmore's life in the White House.

Whitney, David C. *The American Presidents: Biographies of Chief Executives from Washington through Nixon.* New York: Doubleday, 1967. This book provides concise biographies of all the Presidents, from Washington to Nixon, including Fillmore.

Index

PRESIDENTS OF THE UNITED STATES

GEORGE WASHINGTON	L. Falkof	0-944483-19-4
JOHN ADAMS	R. Stefoff	0-944483-10-0
THOMAS JEFFERSON	R. Stefoff	0-944483-07-0
JAMES MADISON	B. Polikoff	0-944483-22-4
JAMES MONROE	R. Stefoff	0-944483-11-9
JOHN QUINCY ADAMS	M. Greenblatt	0-944483-21-6
ANDREW JACKSON	R. Stefoff	0-944483-08-9
MARTIN VAN BUREN	R. Ellis	0-944483-12-7
WILLIAM HENRY HARRISON	R. Stefoff	0-944483-54-2
JOHN TYLER	L. Falkof	0-944483-60-7
JAMES K. POLK	M. Greenblatt	0-944483-04-6
ZACHARY TAYLOR	D. Collins	0-944483-17-8
MILLARD FILLMORE	K. Law	0-944483-61-5
FRANKLIN PIERCE	F. Brown	0-944483-25-9
JAMES BUCHANAN	D. Collins	0-944483-62-3
ABRAHAM LINCOLN	R. Stefoff	0-944483-14-3
ANDREW JOHNSON	R. Stevens	0-944483-16-X
ULYSSES S. GRANT	L. Falkof	0-944483-02-X
RUTHERFORD B. HAYES	N. Robbins	0-944483-23-2
JAMES A. GARFIELD	F. Brown	0-944483-63-1
CHESTER A. ARTHUR	R. Stevens	0-944483-05-4
GROVER CLEVELAND	D. Collins	0-944483-01-1
BENJAMIN HARRISON	R. Stevens	0-944483-15-1
WILLIAM McKINLEY	D. Collins	0-944483-55-0
THEODORE ROOSEVELT	R. Stefoff	0-944483-09-7
WILLIAM H. TAFT	L. Falkof	0-944483-56-9
WOODROW WILSON	D. Collins	0-944483-18-6
WARREN G. HARDING	A. Canadeo	0-944483-64-X
CALVIN COOLIDGE	R. Stevens	0-944483-57-7

HERBERT C. HOOVER	B. Polikoff	0-944483-58-5
FRANKLIN D. ROOSEVELT	M. Greenblatt	0-944483-06-2
HARRY S. TRUMAN	D. Collins	0-944483-00-3
DWIGHT D. EISENHOWER	R. Ellis	0-944483-13-5
JOHN F. KENNEDY	L. Falkof	0-944483-03-8
LYNDON B. JOHNSON	L. Falkof	0-944483-20-8
RICHARD M. NIXON	R. Stefoff	0-944483-59-3
GERALD R. FORD	D. Collins	0-944483-65-8
JAMES E. CARTER	D. Richman	0-944483-24-0
RONALD W. REAGAN	N. Robbins	0-944483-66-6
GEORGE H.W. BUSH	R. Stefoff	0-944483-67-4

GARRETT EDUCATIONAL CORPORATION
130 EAST 13TH STREET
ADA, OK 74820